Robert Frost
Speaking
on Campus

ROBERT FROST

SPEAKING ON CAMPUS

excerpts from his talks

1949–1962

Edited by

Edward Connery Lathem

Introduced by

David M. Shribman

W. W. NORTON & COMPANY

New York · London

MEMENTO MORI

Edward Hyde Cox

1914–1998

Printed in the United States of America
First Edition

For information about permission to reproduce selections from this book,
write to Permissions, W. W. Norton & Company, Inc., 500 Fifth Avenue,
New York, NY 10110.

For information about special discounts for bulk
purchases, please contact W. W. Norton Special Sales at
specialsales@wwnorton.com or 800-233-4830

Manufacturing by RR Donnelley, Harrisonburg

LIBRARY OF CONGRESS CATALOGING-IN-PUBLICATION DATA

Frost, Robert, 1874–1963.

[Speeches. Selections] Robert Frost speaking on campus :
excerpts from his talks, 1949–1962 / edited by Edward Connery Lathem ;
introduced by David M. Shribman.
— 1st ed.   p. cm.
Includes bibliographical references and index.
ISBN 978-0-393-07123-8
1. Speeches, addresses, etc., American. I. Lathem, Edward Connery.
II. Title.
PS3511.R94A6 2009
818'.52—DC22

2009009082

W. W. Norton & Company, Inc.
500 Fifth Avenue, New York, N.Y. 10110
www.wwnorton.com

W. W. Norton & Company Ltd.
Castle House, 75/76 Wells Street, London W1T 3QT

1 2 3 4 5 6 7 8 9 0

Contents

Introduction by David M. Shribman

ROBERT FROST was America's preeminent poet, the winner of four Pulitzer Prizes, the most of any poet. He was called by *The Times* of London, in its obituary announcing his death in 1963, "undoubtedly the most widely known and loved literary figure in America"—to which the paper added, in a separate editorial tribute, that his fame in England was such that, in mourning, "we are also regretting a loss that feels to have happened at home." The President of the United States said of him that he had left "a vacancy in the American spirit": "His death impoverishes us all; but he has bequeathed his nation a body of imperishable verse from which Americans will forever gain joy and understanding." A year earlier, within an introduction for the British edition of Frost's final book of new poems, England's Robert Graves had declared, "The truth is that Frost was the first American who could be honestly reckoned a master-poet by world standards."

During the course of a career that spanned nearly a full half-century—from his first published book, in 1914, until his death—Robert Frost attained immense prominence and popularity as a poet and man of letters. He was that rarity in literary life, celebrated by the general public and scholars alike. He was another rarity, too, an achievement matched in his century perhaps only by William Faulkner: a writer of high art inextricably bound to one region, but nonetheless inarguably regarded as national—even universal.

He was a poet of rural byways, at a time when the nation was building urban and interstate highways. He was a high priest of the leisure thought, at a time when the country worshipped the hurry of commerce. His focus often was on agriculture and the pastoral, at the high tide of industry. He seemed sturdily to be a remnant of the past, in a world that prayed at the altar of the future. He articulated big truths, in a century that perfected the big lie.

Yet Frost, the countryman in a country of cities and an apparent antique in the culture of the new, was as current as the morning newspaper, with mass appeal in the first mass-market, mass-culture nation. He appeared on the covers of literary magazines, such as *The Atlantic Monthly* and *Saturday Review*, but also on the covers of popular mega-circulation magazines, such as *Time* and *Life*. He was both well-regarded and well-loved.

As the years passed, awards flowed to him, cascaded in upon him. He was given more than forty honorary degrees, including ones from both Oxford and Cambridge, a dual tribute that had been accorded but two American writers before him, Henry Wadsworth Longfellow and James Russell Lowell, back in the nineteenth century. A mountain was named for him in his home state of Vermont. A unanimous vote of Congress, which had previously saluted him with formal resolutions on his seventy-fifth and eighty-fifth birthdays, led to the striking in his honor of a special gold medal, presented to him in 1962 on his eighty-eighth birthday. All this for a man who, as expressed in his poem "A Considerable Speck," had "none of the tenderer-than-thou / Collectivistic regimenting love / With which the modern world is being swept."

Frost from time to time retreated to the farm, but never was a hermit. Increasingly over the years, he became a public man — a personage. And it was not too much to say that, as such, he embraced the public and it embraced him. During the closing period of his life, he referred to the "publicality" of his existence — the word is his, as was the profile. But this publicality wasn't something he took on only in grandfatherly old age (and indeed there was much to Frost, early and late, that was not grandfatherly, for his was a world of conflict, not confection). However, his role as a public figure was perhaps underlined by his appointment in 1958 as Consultant in Poetry at the Library

of Congress — equivalent to designation as Poet Laureate of the United States — and being thereafter the Lbrary's Honorary Consultant in the Humanities.

During March of 1962, slightly more than a year after his having dramatically played a cameo role in John F. Kennedy's presidential inauguration, he told a Florida interviewer: "I've been publicized more this year than ever in my life. It turns me outside in, or inside out. So much pleasant attention. But on the outside, that isn't where you write poetry."

For a man who was a student of the inner life, and who stirred the inner life of the public, being out in public was ironic, and he himself was struck by the many ironies it prompted. He went to the Soviet Union that year of 1962, engaging while there in an historic, much-publicized one-on-one meeting with Premier Nikita Khrushchev. (He had earlier been on cultural goodwill missions, also arranged by the State Department, to several countries: Brazil, Great Britain, Ireland, Israel, and Greece.) Later, to an Amherst College audience he said of his Soviet trip: "My career as a teacher and as a writer has almost been wiped out by my going to Russia. I haven't met anybody lately that doesn't know I've been to Russia, though they've never read one of my books."

Robert Frost's poetry has survived him, and in truth appears to have grown in renown. "The utmost of ambition is," he wrote in a tribute to his fellow poet Edwin Arlington Robinson, "to lodge a few poems where they will be hard to get rid of. . . ." Clearly, by that gauge, Frost's own poetic ambition has been monumentally realized and his reputation as a poet rendered amply secure.

But most readers today do not know Frost — have had no way of knowing him — in one of his most important roles, as teacher and lecturer. He was in fact one of America's great teachers, one of its great presences as such, in a classroom or on a platform or stage. Although many years, many decades, have passed, there do remain today some for whom the memory of Robert Frost on an academic campus — college or university or preparatory school — endures with a special power and vividness, both intellectual and visual. He did with frequency speak elsewhere, before groups of various sorts and to general audiences, in cities and towns all across the land. But his academic audiences were those he liked best.

He himself had run away from colleges — most notably, as an undergraduate, from both Dartmouth and Harvard. ("Dartmouth is my chief college," he told an interviewer in 1960, "the first one I ran away from. I ran from Harvard later, but Dartmouth first." And sometimes he would add, as he did at Connecticut College in 1961, "Dartmouth's where I began my career, by running away.") However, he ran to colleges as well, acknowledging that they were the oxygen of poetry in America. "I wouldn't be here, I wouldn't be in existence if it hadn't been for patronage of colleges," he said while speaking to a college audience in May of 1954, and exaggerating only slightly. "In America we don't have any lords and ladies to patronize poets. And so we have to depend on colleges and the audiences that they give us. One of the best audiences the world ever had is what I call a mixed town-and-gown audience in a college town. And that's what's given me my life, my living."

Frost had a term for his literary peregrinations; he called them "barding around," which is a nice phrase, perhaps a bit self-aggrandizing even as it is possessed of a playful self-effacing tone. To Frost, barding around was what poets did—what he himself did from sea to sea, as well as sometimes across an ocean. And by barding around he was bonding with a great tradition. "That's the way the poet does his begging, you know," he said to the students at Choate School in 1962. "Ever since Homer we were beggars." And he went on to quote lines from a Thomas Seward poem that read: "Seven wealthy towns contend for Homer dead, / Through which the living Homer begged his bread." Then, he confided: "I've begged my way through more than that. I 'get around,' as they say, with these poems. And it's all in such a nice American way."

Even when his presentations to an audience were to be essentially a reading of his poetry, he would typically begin, like an opera, with an overture, talking informally. As he said in explanation at the University of Miami in 1960: "I permit myself one free-verse poem, extempore, to begin with. . . . It is some little theme I have—sometimes political, sometimes religious, sometimes historical. It's about something I've just arrived at." Similarly, at the University of Iowa in 1959, he told his audience: "I begin with a little talk like this, as my only free verse. I don't write free verse. I talk free verse, extempore." But even speaking extemporaneously, he came through as the sage of the written page.

Over the years, Frost as teacher became a masterly figure, in classrooms, lecture halls, and auditoriums — before audiences consisting of students in but a single academic course or before a throng of listeners. (More than eighty-five hundred attended what, at the University of Detroit in November of 1962, would prove to be one of his last platform appearances.) He was a showman, and he was good at it, and he knew it. "He is, in fact," wrote poet-critic-translator John Ciardi of Frost, in a *Saturday Review* article, "a king of the old pros: he knows how to tickle an audience and he knows how to knock it for a loop."

But it hadn't always been that way. For Frost the stage was an acquired taste, and an acquired skill, hard-fought for and hard-won. In his early years he was terrified of being before an audience, and part of the Frost life narrative, as told by his official biographer, Lawrance Thompson, is of how he was consumed with fright when he was to deliver his valedictory address at the Lawrence, Massachusetts, high school in 1892. Thompson relates that Frost, "unbearably nervous," dashed from the stage shortly before he was scheduled to speak, ran down the auditorium's back stairwell, soaked his handkerchief in a sink, drenched his face in cold water, paced in the hall's lower corridor, and finally crept back — almost paralyzed with trepidation — to his place on the stage, there to face the excruciating ordeal of speaking.

Twice, in 1906 and in 1907, he was filled with such dread at the prospect of reading a poem of his aloud to the Men's League of the Congregational Church in Derry, New Hampshire, that the pastor had to read his work for him. In 1909, when called upon to address a group of fellow teachers, he placed pebbles in his shoes, in the hope that the discomfort in his feet would distract him from his fear. And Thompson provides this account of Frost's appearing before a group in Boston a half-dozen years later, just after his return from England and the publication of his first two books:

"Having determined to suffer whatever the cost to his nerves, so that he might improve his own poetic stature through making such public appearances, he had done his best to assert courage, boldness, daring. Yet when he had stood up to speak before the audience at the Authors' Club his hands had trembled so much that he had feared he would drop the book he held. Before he had uttered a single word he could feel his lips trembling, and his voice had actually quavered, noticeably. He had seen that some of his listeners were suffering with him."

Frost never really mastered his stage fright, only controlled it. A third of a century later, in the postscript to a letter to the editor of the *Amherst Graduates' Quarterly*, in a declaration only partly in jest, he wrote: "The only reason I go on the platform at all is to show my bravery. . . . I do it to make up for never having faced bullets like the real hero. I suffer more before and after than during action."

But once he had controlled his stage fright, he managed to make the stage his friend, in part because it had become for him a pulpit. He found inspiration there, in the pulpit, and his performances from the pulpit were in many cases inspiring. There he was able to project what he called "the nicety of words" as eloquently from his lips as he could from his pen. In the pulpit, as if on a mountain summit, he sometimes spoke as someone who had — as he put it in an entirely different context in a poem titled, pointedly, "Reluctance" — "climbed the hills of view / And looked at the world, and descended." His was a life designed to "say back to the world" — even if he wasn't at any given moment quite sure exactly what he would say. And in the pulpit that is what he did, incomparably and unforgettably.

The ease with which he approached the speaking arts can be measured by the ease with which in his talks he often wandered, no longer sustainingly subject to the muse on any given topic, but actually just musing about this and that. Even when Frost was invited to deliver a set-piece lecture or a commencement address, he spoke informally, without a prepared manuscript or notes of any kind, and did not resist the impulse to roam in his remarks into rhetorical roads not previously taken or roads unexpected and, in some cases, roads quite random.

There were sometimes occasions when Frost, he having beforehand provided a title for his talk, would appear and speak about something else entirely. Once, in the spring of 1954, when he had been listed on a college course syllabus to speak on "The Natural and Supernatural Bounds of Science," he began his talk by saying, "You've had that, the name of the lecture, so long in front of you that I think you've probably figured out for yourselves what it was to be about, so I'll talk about something else." And he did. At a Washington press conference in 1960 he said: "It always is a mystery about what I'm going to say to anybody about anything until I see the whites of their eyes. Only this year they asked me out in Ohio, Columbus, if I'd give them a choice of three subjects. I haven't got three subjects. No choice; they have to take what they get from me. . . ."

Though lighthearted or casual, whimsical or capricious, as

they sometimes might seem to be, Frost never took his speaking engagements lightly. "Mr. Frost likes very much to be left entirely alone before he is going to speak," H. Bacon Collamore in 1938 advised a prospective host of the poet. "In other words, if you are

going to have him talk in the evening he likes to go somewhere and rest and not have to say a word to anybody. Also, he eats a very light supper before talking. This usually consists of a cup of warm milk and one or two raw eggs. . . . He just hates to have someone give a dinner for him prior to his talking, which makes it necessary for him to carry on a conversation with people. It upsets him dreadfully."

But for all the edginess of the hours leading to a talk, the performance itself typically had an easy air. The transformation had come slowly for a man who in his earliest public engagements had, verging on panic, sped through his presentations — "in terror of my life," as he in 1950 described to a Tufts audience his experience there at the college in 1915 when he read two of his poems to its Phi Beta Kappa chapter: "like a rabbit scuttling . . . , without any awareness of what I was doing; just got through it alive."

Once, however, the transformation from terrified reader to in-control speaker had been achieved, his listeners were provided with a rich complement to his poetry, not merely an occasion to compliment his poems. Though what he had to say was not written down, it was not off-the-cuff either. He was informal, but not improvisional. He may have seemed to have been a stream-of-thought speaker, but his speaking waters ran deep, not shallow, and his presentation was generally masterful. "A deceptive air of nonchalance might lead the uninitiated to assume that he regards lecturing lightly," his friend Reginald Cook, who had many times heard Frost address various audiences, wrote of him in 1956. "But the facts point to an opposite conclusion."

Poetry is of course meant to be spoken, as well as to be read — Frost would in the course of his "barding around" tell his audiences that he wanted to "say" some of his poems — and there was special interest in hearing him say the poems aloud and also in what he had to say about them. But supplementing that — surrounding it and enriching it — was the particular interest associated with hearing the "free-verse poem, extempore, to begin with" that usually was a part of his presentation — hearing that and the comments and observations he interspersed with "saying" the poetry.

What he imparted to his listeners was typically conveyed in the spirit of three words of invitation, drawn from his *North of Boston* poem "The Pasture" (the poem used by him as the introductory element for each of his comprehensive collected editions): "You come too."

It was an invitation that related to a broad sphere of subject coverage — to, as expressed within the dedication statement of one of his books, "range beyond range even into the realm of government and religion." And the way in which what was conveyed was expressed was an affirmation of what might be called Robert Frost's "Iron Rule of Language": that — as is declared in his poem "The Mountain" — " . . . all the fun's in how you say a thing."

It was one of the great writer/talkers, Mark Twain (like Frost both a literary and public figure, beloved both in America and in England), who drew a distinction between speeches and talks, and who declared that "*speeches* can be conveyed in print, but not *talks*." He asserted that whereas speeches consist of carefully crafted sentences and the rounded expression of thought

precisely communicated, such is not characteristically so with talks. "The soul of a talk," he held, "consists of action," not simply words — action that included gestures and vocal inflection; "the unvoiced expression of the thought" — all of which is uncapturable by a stenographer's record of what is uttered.

But Mark Twain to the contrary notwithstanding, there can be great value in collecting and presenting in printed form talks given by certain speakers. Talk is not always cheap; often it is exceedingly rich — especially when, as in the case of both Twain (whose talks have in fact been posthumously published) and Frost, it emanates from a master of both the written and spoken language. In its spontaneity — whether totally spontaneous or in greater or lesser degree so — it can convey not just what its speaker thinks, but how the speaker thinks. A talk is not simply the product of thought, it can also reveal significantly the process of thought.

Robert Frost thought in serenity, but he thought out loud, as well. And it is clear that from an early period — reaching back to the teens and the nineteen-twenties — he himself was concerned about there existing a record of at least some of what he expressed in talk. Writing in 1932 to his friend Sidney Cox, he explicitly focused upon the matter of possible talk-based publication: "I'll tell you my notion of the contract you thought you had with me. The objective idea is all I ever cared about. Most of my ideas occur in verse. But I have always had some turning up in talk that I feared I might never use because I was too lazy to write prose. I think they have been mostly educational ideas connected with my teaching, actually lessons. That's where I hoped you would come in. I thought if it didn't take you too much from your own affairs you might be willing to gather them for us both."

A year and a half later, he is found writing again to Cox: "I didn't mean exactly what you thought I did when years ago I was so incautious as to suggest that you might like to turn to account some of the theories of school, life, and art I let fall in talk but was too lazy ever probably to use in writing myself. You took it that I was asking to be Boswellized. . . . I meant something the most impersonal." And farther along in this same letter, he added: "I shrink from prefaces as you know. Once in a while it comes over me to wish some friend would do my explaining for me. It shouldnt take much and it might better be based on my talk in general than on particular rambling talks with me."

A few of Frost's talks were published during his lifetime, some with his permission, some without. At Amherst while it was his academic home base in the early nineteen-thirties and again in the late nineteen-forties, two of his talks were brought out in the *Amherst Graduates' Quarterly*, and in both instances Frost revised them himself prior to publication. In the earlier of the two cases (1931), he first made handwritten emendations, some of them extensive, to each of the twenty-two pages of the stenographic transcript; then subsequently he entered further changes to all of the pages of the typescript that represented his initial revision. And in the latter instance of publication (1948), he began what he wrote to the *Quarterly*'s editor about that text's revision: "The temptation is to go even further than you with this and round it into a real piece. But perhaps that wouldn't be fair to those who heard it as a speech or talk. They might feel bamboozled. It hurts like everything not to bring my point out more sharply."

Actually, Frost always found it exceedingly difficult to bring himself to revise his spoken texts. He failed, for example, to fulfill his contract to revise for publication his six Charles Eliot Norton Lectures at Harvard in 1936. He evidently didn't even open the package of stenographic transcripts of them that was sent to him from Harvard University Press, and Lawrance Thompson speculates that he finally simply burned them. Two decades later, in 1956, the Fund for the Republic succeeded in securing his permission to publish the commencement address he had delivered that year at Sarah Lawrence College, and it was issued as a booklet entitled *A Talk for Students*. In his letter granting consent, however, Frost stressed that his remarks were to be regarded as "just talk," made "without notes," and were "not an essay written."

There was one occasion when Frost, late in life, engaged actively in a quite comprehensive revision of one of his talks, the speech he delivered in 1959 when he received the Emerson–Thoreau Medal from the American Academy of Arts and Sciences. His topic then was Emerson, whom he admired deeply, and the attention he lavished, following its delivery, upon that text was undoubtedly a measure of his special regard for his subject.

Robert Frost's performances — the word is not chosen lightly; Frost was a "performance artist" before the term existed — were for both the eye and the ear. As Reginald Cook observed in his 1956 article "Notes on Frost the Lecturer": "The voice, although a major part of the play, is augmented by the constant gesture of the hands, the frequent nod of the head, the changing facial expression, and even the stance, squared away, confronting his auditors, and depending very much upon the feel of the group. What the human aspects — the voice, gesture, expression, and appearance — represent is a natural presence not soon forgotten. Frost behaves as he looks. You never see him when he affects the poet, and you never hear him when he isn't one."

His audiences, small or large, unquestionably knew they were experiencing the "natural presence" of someone of consequence. And that knowledge, shared by speaker and listener alike, forged the initial bond that, by a given occasion's end, tended to link them inextricably — a link strengthened because in an auditorium Frost always preferred to have the house lights left on, in order that he might clearly see his listeners.

As he addressed his audience, frequently he hesitated; often he was tentative. His talks are full of small asides. He varied the tempo of his remarks with the speed of his mind. In this regard, Peter J. Stanlis, a friend who knew Frost well as a talker in various settings, informal and formal, wrote of him for one of the volumes of *Frost Centennial Essays*: "He often gave the impression that he was thinking out loud and improvising as he rambled on from point to point, even from phrase to phrase, with pauses between points and phrases, while he visibly probed his mind, fishing out from some dim recess an original idea, image, or analogy, which became reflected in his face and gestures, as the idea, image, or analogy welled up inside him and spurted out of his mouth in a voice that also seemed to be searching for exactly the right word and tone to convey it directly to each listener."

With an easy air, mixing ideas and idiom freely, he often

shifted into the vernacular. He wasn't above shortening "because" to "'cause" or "them" to "'em" or "so as" to "so's" — or saying "gotta" and "'tis" and "'tisn't." For effect he would even occasionally employ decidedly slangy expression, such as "That don't mean . . ." and "Ain't it hell. . . ."

His manner was, in a word, conversational. And because conversation is an auditory medium, not a written one — and, whenever face-to-face with those being talked to, can be very much a visual one as well — the true texture of what Frost said, the total effect of precisely how he conveyed what he uttered, cannot be fully captured, it must be conceded, on a printed page. Mark Twain was, a century ago when dictating his autobiography, surely right in asserting that. And the editor of talks undoubtedly has frequent occasion to echo, in this respect, Frost's own revisional lament of nearly three score years ago: "It hurts like everything not to bring my [Frost's] point out more sharply."

An editor in bringing forth a talk's text for publication cannot undertake to sprinkle it with bracketed indications (as in a script for actors learning lines of dialogue) of the way in which something is said: earnestly, casually, jokingly, and the like. A clear-cut example, from within this volume, of a statement by

Frost that could potentially be misunderstood or misinterpreted when read is provided within his 1956 talk at the University of Oregon. Toward the beginning of his comments, he spoke elliptically about his philosophy of teaching, as well as about writing, and he then added what might seem to a reader an odd, jarring interjection: "That's a curious thing in our day, speaking of the different kinds of people who set up to be as important as I am." In this case, as in others, a transcript can't reproduce the tone of voice and facial expression that at the time of the sentence's delivery the audience on that April evening in Eugene readily understood to be one of self-mocking jest.

In like fashion, the printed page cannot be made to carry and impart in any at all adequate degree the humor that attended Frost's manner of telling, in a January 1960 talk that is also represented in these pages, of a taunting exchange that had been engaged in between himself and an inebriated fellow poet — an account in which his mimicry of the slurred speech that was involved ("I imitated his manner.") produced amusement to his listeners.

On the pages that follow are included excerpts from forty-six talks, as delivered at thirty-two academic institutions in the period 1949 to 1962, the final fourteen years of Robert Frost's life. There is a preponderance of talks given at Dartmouth, in part because Frost made an annual appearance there before the college's storied Great Issues Course, in which the presentations by guest lecturers were routinely tape-recorded, this in an era when such recording elsewhere was not so common as it would later become.

It might be noted that Frost's talks were oftentimes studded with quotations from the verse of others, poets both American and British, quoted by him entirely from memory and with a remarkable degree of accuracy. He did, however, now and again, as readers of what follows may discover, lapse in the verbatim recollection of texts that he with seeming ease brought to mind and recited. (During a July 1955 session with students at the Bread Loaf School of English, he asked, "Did you ever notice

this about your memory, that in the course of years you corrupt a line in poetry in a pretty fair way until it's got to be something else with you entirely?")

He even on rare occasion faltered with his own poetry, even indeed with so familiar a poem as "Birches"—of which he told an audience at the Library of Congress in 1955: "I know that by heart, but I know it so well, I sometimes forget it in the middle of it. . . . I made a mistake with it the last time I said it." And as well as he knew Emerson's poetry, he on at least some occasions rendered the closing stanza of "Give All to Love" as beginning "Verily know . . . ," instead of "Heartily know. . . ."

In addition, he sometimes was, as is evident on the pages that follow, forgetful or merely casual in making reference to the titles of published works — with Henry George's *Progress and Poverty* transposed to *Poverty and Progress*, the "Federalist Papers" becoming the "Federal Papers," and "The Hollow Men" cited as "The Hollow Man." Nor were his own poems exempt from an occasional careless naming of them, as in "A Tuft of Flowers" for "The Tuft of Flowers." All matters of no particular consequence — seemingly not to him and certainly not to his listeners.

There are many lessons in this volume, some about Frost, some about poetry, some about life, and some about how Frost, poetry, and life help explain one another. Certainly paramount among the lessons here is that Frost was a poet by profession, but fundamentally and always a teacher by temperament. He mixed the two, both in his poetry and in his public appearances — in his readings and his talks — and most especially when on an academic campus. He was never one without being also the other: poet and teacher.

"The business of the teacher is, I presume, to challenge the student's purpose," Frost said in an interview published during December of 1925 in *The Christian Science Monitor*, an interview in which he described his teaching method as being "education by presence." (It is a description or characterization that should be especially evocative to those who dip into or linger over the pages of this volume.) ". . . I do not mean," he explained, "the challenge should be made in words. That, I should think, is nearly fruitless." And he went on to declare: ". . . I am an indifferent teacher as teachers go, and it is hard to understand why I am wanted around colleges unless there is some force it is thought I can exert by merely belonging to them. It must be that what I stand for does my work."

In one of the talks from which an excerpt is included in this volume, drawn from an afternoon's presentation at Harvard in 1956, Frost notes the link within his own life between conversation and education, and he quotes two lines of his verse that as subsequently published read: "It takes all sorts of in- and outdoor schooling / To get adapted to my kind of fooling." Much of Frost's poetry is set outdoors, while almost all of his teaching occurred of course indoors. To see Frost whole, one needs to examine the outdoor man when he was indoors. And no places indoors give us in this regard the opportunity for so many insights concerning him as do college, university, or preparatory school classrooms and lecture halls — the places within which over the years he spoke to many thousand students, as well as to others in those town-and-gown audiences he liked so well.

In some notebook jottings of his, published in *The Atlantic Monthly* in 1951 under the title "Poetry and School," there are tucked into the middle of a paragraph two sentences that combine his outdoor genius with his indoor genius, lines that are poignant to us today: "The best educated person is one who has been matured at just the proper rate. Seasoned but not kiln dried." What Frost said in the previously unpublished talks that are represented here, some of them now more than a half-century old, most of them all but forgotten, may perhaps be thought of as having now, with the passing of time, matured for us at just the proper rate. Turn the pages of this book and you can discover for yourself: They are seasoned, and not kiln dried.

David Shribman

**Robert Frost
Speaking
on Campus**

Getting up things to say for yourself

One of the elements of Robert Frost's longtime association with Dartmouth College was his annual participation as a guest lecturer, from the late-1940s onward, in the college's Great Issues Course, a required component of the curriculum for all Dartmouth seniors. Here presented are excerpts from his April 11, 1949, lecture to the class, a talk that was entitled "Some Obstinacy."

THE FIRST THING to say is that you've got to start getting up things to say for yourself, if you want to hold your own. And the pre-first thing to say is that you gotta have an own to hold. And you can have that any way you please. You can call it "pre-conception" or "prejudice." But it's something that you'd rather have so than not — either about God or man or education or science — something you'd rather have so than not. If it's no matter to you, it'd be hard for me to talk to you. There'd be nothing for me to talk up against. [. . .]

Now, when I say "get up something to say for yourself," that's the important thing. Somewhere you've got to start that, getting up things to say for yourself, if you want to hold your own. [. . .]

Some obstinacy is important. But it's rather dull simply to hold your own from sheer stubbornness. But that's better than nothing.

Suppose you come here pronouncing a word a certain way. Will you give it up for the first professor that doesn't pronounce it that way? No, your answer will be: "In my family, we say it this way: We don't say 'ab'·do·men' in my family, we say 'ab·do'·men'."

Or vice versa. You don't give up. "We drop the t in 'kept' in my family, and we put it onto 'acrosst'."

And before you give that up, you look into it, see what the history of all that is. How did that come into our speech, that dropping the t and putting it on somewhere else? Stubbornly — to begin with — you'll stubbornly look into it; let's see a minute.

That's a slight matter. But it's always a bad sign to me when people come home from college, after two or three months, correcting their family about everything — pronunciation and all that — bad sign, getting educated too easily.

When I look back over my life, I can remember when I first began getting up something to hold my own with, when I thought just stubbornness seemed rather stupid, wasn't exciting enough, wasn't fun enough. I had to get up a "rigmarole." You see, you've got to get up a rigmarole. Don't be afraid of the word. Get up a rigmarole.

And I'm going to get up and show you some rigmaroles I've got up for my own defense, for the defense of my position, in the course of the years — in the defense of my friends' positions sometimes.

One of the first ones I remember was for my mother, to help her. She encountered the idea that we were descended from monkeys. This was back in the seventies and eighties — eighties, way back then. (I remember the first time I heard of "the missing link." I saw it in the newspaper in San Francisco and had to have it explained to me.) But I remember saying to her shortly after that — (I've forgotten how old I was; high-school age.) — that I didn't see that it made much difference whether God made man out of mud, as it says in the Bible, or out of prepared mud, as Darwin says; it's just worked up a little.

And the other day I heard something better than that. (That's had a long history for me.) I heard that the virus — that we talk about so much, when we don't know any better — the virus is very close to crystal form. It was shown this way. [. . .] The disease called "mosaic" on potatoes, when boiled down and then dried out to crystalize, and then boiled again and crystalized, and then boiled again and crystalized would still give the mosaic to potatoes. And it made my biological friend suspicious that there must be some very close connection between the beginning of life in virus and crystals. So, maybe God made us out of crystals, you see — a little rigmarole.

Now, a course like this is churns the place up, clear down to the depths where I am; reached me. And it's kept me thinking about issues all this winter. I've been at about twenty colleges, and I've been talking "great issues" or somewhere near 'em. It's helped me earn my living. And I'm going to speak of two or three that I've talked about, and then come to one very serious one, one that is still a rigmarole in my handling of it.

I always get around 'em with some little story — (A little "song and dance," you might call it.) — some way, some line of verse. One of them, for instance: There was a Puritan in the old days — (I believe T. S. Eliot has discovered that he wasn't a Puritan, but he *was* a Puritan.) — and he was the second greatest poet of the British. His name was Milton. And he'd been brought up to think that works were important — to work, to serve was important. And he came on a conflict of ideas.

He heard of the people that talked about "works" and "faith without works," and he saw an issue there. And he himself was thrown into trouble about the issue, the unresolved issue.

You see, it still stands. One great poet says:

> The truth is great, and shall prevail,
> When none cares whether it prevail or not.[1]

You don't have to do anything about it, about doing good. One of the great poets says that:

> The truth is great, and shall prevail,
> When none cares whether it prevail or not.

But Milton couldn't believe that. He thought you had to care for the truth and work for it. And then he lost the instrument of his works, his sight. He looked for a moment as if he'd got the worst of that argument, between works and no works, faith without works. And he got up a rigmarole — just like me. He wrote a whole sonnet to end up, "They also serve who only stand and waite."[2] And he was out. He had the conflict resolved, you see.

Lately — another one — I just came across a book by a young follower of an old philosopher out at Wisconsin. [. . .] One of his followers has just written a book to show that people waste their time thinking about a hereafter. It's a godless book, perfectly godless. He's thrown God out, and he's thrown the future out. It's an elaborate book, and it's called *Hello, Man*. (He's just discovered man and said "hello" to him; seen him coming down the street!)

Now, that's on one side of one of these great issues. [. . .] That's speaking of man as if he were the whole thing and had this world and nothing else — no God, no future. And here's somebody says of this man:

> Great lord of all things, yet a prey to all;
> Sole judge of Truth, in endless Error hurled:
> The glory, jest, and riddle of the world![3]

That's man the failure, or man at once the success and failure. Another poem that would go well with that says:

> I know my life's a pain and but a span;
> I know my sense is mock'd in everything;
> And, to conclude, I know myself a Man —
> Which is a proud and yet a wretched thing.

Let's see, there's another stanza that I might remember of that. It says:

> I know my soul has power to know all things,

> Yet is she blind and ignorant in all.
> I know I'm one of Nature's little kings,
> Yet to the least and vilest things am thrall.[4]

Now, that brings you in conflict. Here's somebody who says that this life is enough, man is enough, the brotherhood of man is enough, and that man is sufficient to himself; and if you can't get enough comfort, pleasure, and happiness out of that, why talk about it. And then here's a whole realm of literature — religious literature and semi-religious literature — that says this life, man's condition, is like that:

> I know my life's a pain and but a span;
> I know my sense is mock'd in everything;
> And, to conclude, I know myself a Man —
> Which is a proud and yet a wretched thing.

Well, you have those two things, and I've put those two things together in one of my Great Issues talks. I'm getting on to the one I want to emphasize most.

Down at Technology they are telling us that man is about to conquer space. (I saw it in the Saturday edition of the *Christian Science Monitor*. Not Sunday; that comes out Saturday afternoon.) Man is about to conquer space.

They say down there that there's no probable reason why we shouldn't go to the moon, and we might go even further. We might, for the sake of collecting uranium, go to Uranus. (That's a very outlying place, you know. But we want uranium terribly — "terrifically," as the girls say.)

Now, I wouldn't venture to tell science how far it might not go in certain directions. It might go to the moon. It might go to Uranus. And it might make free with all space. (You see, space is limited, anyway, they tell us now; Mr. Einstein tells us.)

But I will venture to show you certain directions where

science can never go. And I've just thought I'd use a line of Shakespeare to do that with, and divide the world between, we'll say, "the spirit of man" and science, the scientific. I don't like to say "the spiritual," because you'll think I mean something religious. But I mean to include religion and poetry and the arts. And I'll make it even a lesser thing than that: our human personal relations. [. . .]

Now, just do it with one line of Shakespeare — divide the world for you in equal halves. I have to say four lines to get to the one I want. The lines go like this:

> O no; it is an ever-fixed mark,
> That looks on tempests, and is never shaken;
> It is the star to every wandering bark . . .

And now the line:

> Whose worth's unknown, although its
> height be taken.[5]

Shakespeare divides the world, you see there, very prettily. The star — the North Star that brings the traveler home, that brings the ship home — is of untold worth, inestimable worth. Science will never touch it. It'll bring home some people that ought not to come home, won't it? And then, on the other side, the exactness of science: whose worth's unknown, although its height be exactly taken. There you have the two, the divided world.

Now, everything I've said, all the issues I've spoken of, are on that left-hand side that I've divided the world into — on the spirit-of-man side, the spiritual side — all that I have spoken of.

Take one that concerns me very deeply, between free verse and the kind of verse I think I write. (I'm in the *Dictionary of American Biography* as a free-verse writer. I've tried to get that out, and they won't take it out. Let it stay in. There's an issue there!)

8

As a matter of fact, that comes up, and I have to get up something to say to hold my own to Carl Sandburg, my friend Carl Sandburg. And I say to him, "I'd as soon write free verse as play tennis with the net down." You see? And after a year or two of thinking that over, he comes back and says, "Couldn't you play better tennis with the net down?"

And then — carries it over to the spiritual side, the non-scientific side — the question comes up: Isn't free verse playful enough — in making phrases and using words the way they ought to be; isn't there enough play in that, enough of art in that — without going in for rhyme and metre? And what you lose, in playfulness in rhyme and metre, don't you gain in sincerity — a thing they call "sincerity" — which is beyond the reach of science, outside the range of science?

I'd like to take that away from seeming at all mysterious, if I could. And so I'll take another place in Shakespeare to show you where science will never come.

Let me never hear you, in my presence, anyway — "let you never say," as the Irish say — let you never say in my presence that science may shrug today at a lot of things it can't touch, but it'll get around to them someday, you know. It's a condescending shrug; it means to come around someday. And they're saying that down at the school of technology. They're saying it, that everything can someday, you know.

Well, let's name something else, if I can. Let's take something very, very small and very specific. Shakespeare says, "Most friendship is feigning. . . ."[6] First thing you say to him is: "Aren't you exaggerating that a little? Need you say 'most'? Say 'some'; use some measure, be moderate in it."

"All right," he says, "*some* friendship is feigning." Any help from science about that? What friendship is feigning?

I look somebody in the eyes, and we look together hard at

each other and we think, "How long will we stand each other, and keep up this pretense, for what we can get out of it?" And how low that is. But how very difficult it is.

What do you know about truth? Truth is less important to me, always, than just plain trueness. How do I judge anyone's true friendship, except by my own trueness and untrueness? I know 'em both. And will anybody venture to say that science will ever have anything to do with that? Stays outside.

What's that got to do with comfort? Sure, science has a lot to do with comfort, has a lot to do with pleasure. And then it has something to do with happiness, because they come partly out of comfort and pleasure. But there's this whole realm, you see, where science can't touch you. And your happiness is all there.

He says something worse than that, doesn't he? He says, "Most friendship is feigning, most loving mere folly." Folly; what loving is folly? You don't say, "God only knows!" You go out to judge it by your own trueness and untrueness. You've got nothing else but what you've grown in yourself, your own trueness and untrueness. Not your truth; that's too large for my purpose. But your trueness and untrueness.

Some people have no gift at all that way. They don't know who's fooling 'em. They haven't grown up right. There's something been lacking.

Well, to bring it back to the first thing I said, a little bit — connect it with that. Knowledge we're talking about. [. . .] An old poem says:

> Since Knowledge is but sorrow's Spy,
> It is not safe to know.[7]

I hear many people — kind of cheap talkers, political talkers — say that knowledge will solve everything. If the Russians only knew enough, we could love 'em. And they think if we only knew enough, they could love us. This question of how much knowledge is enough. But here's someone back there — (This is the son of Shakespeare; said to be, you know, putative.) — he says:

Since Knowledge is but sorrow's Spy . . .

That's the biblical sense of "spy": spies out the land, you know. It's sent out to bring on into the land of sorrow; knowledge leads you into the land of sorrow.—

It is not safe to know.

Well, we all know the danger of knowledge. I don't know anything you can't have too much of, even knowledge — even sweetness. How much knowledge is enough?

I don't think there's enough expectation around these colleges that you should start getting up things to say for yourself, to hold your own. The expectation is that you should pick up things to hold your own with — pick up; that knowledge should do it.

But, no; there must be a time. I'd like to set the age. I wish science could help me — I wish the laboratory could help me — tell you when you ought to have a right to expect yourself to get up something to hold your own with — your own being something you want to have so, that you'd like to have proved so. [. . .]

When will you have enough to go ahead with, to do things? Well, our whole setup in this country is as if when you got to be about forty, you might know enough to start doing something. [. . .]

Is it that we don't expect enough of young people? We seem to think that if we fill the basement with oily rags, someday it'll spontaneously combust. But there ain't anything to that.

And I was told when I was young: You learn to write now; you learn the forms of things; you learn what other people have written. Then, if you ever have anything to say when you're forty, you'll know how to say it; you'll start something then.

Of course that's not so. The whole art of writing is learning how to have something to say. You've got to start that. You've got to get up things; get 'em up.

There's probably an issue between me and my fellow teachers right there, some of my fellow teachers. I watch them trying to make the system over — maybe toward that, I don't know; maybe toward my side. They're trying to reassemble the old bones. And it makes me think of another poem. American poem this is. (These are the bones of education, you know, the dry bones of education.) He says, American poet says:

> Then Jones of Calaveras he reconstructed there
> A prehistoric animal that was extremely rare;
> But Brown, he asked the chair for a suspension
> of the rules,
> Till he could prove that those same bones were
> one of his lost mules.[8]

After they've made the colleges over — (I've seen a lot of them this year, and they all seem to have been made over.) — but they look to me like one of my "lost mules." It's the same old creature. All right, leave that there.

Then, another one — another that I've talked about in my travels — is what you might call "the higher treason."

What set me off thinking about it was an article in the *Harper's Magazine*, leading article, on what loyalty would mean in a time like this. And loyalty in a time like this, apparently, would be a kind of a transcendental treason — à la Emerson, à la old man Royce, the old philosopher at Harvard.

Now, let's get that straight. I'll show you how a man slips off into that.

Down in Washington, when Russia was our ally, everybody in the State Department had to be on Russia's side. They all were on Russia's side. But there was a division then. There was an issue, right then. Some were glad to be on Russia's side and some were sorry. They all did their duty, and some were glad to do it and some were sorry.

The division widened when the thing was over, and some went off into what I call "the transcendental treason." They knew something better than their own country. Emerson says:

> Verily know,
> When half-gods go,
> The gods arrive.[9]

Verily know, when the United States goes, there'll be a better country for you somewhere in the world. The world-nation will be better than this. See, "Verily know."

The only thing about that is, as I've observed people who went on that in their relations with each other — ("Verily know, / When half-gods go, / The gods arrive.") — those that left half-gods landed in quarter-gods next, and so on down to eighth-gods. And the last I saw of 'em, one of 'em had got down to a smaller fraction than that, of a god — married to her.

There's a whole book about it by Josiah Royce that leads you off that way. And I'm not going to quote Blackstone, but all you have to do is look at Blackstone to find out what disloyalty is and what treason is. It's very simple. I don't know whether you know or not; it's very simple.

You can muss words all around, talk this stuff of Emerson's. A great admirer of Emerson, I am. But it's a hole in the sky, that is; a hole in the sky — not a hole in the ground, but a hole in the sky.

Somebody asked me what I thought it was. What am I going to say to it, about treason? What is treason? Same thing; I have to get up something to say for myself, to hold my own.

I don't like treason. I like people that belong to this country, in some shape or other. There's quite a variety of us. I'm allowing for plenty of variety.

But my answer to that is: Disloyalty is that for the lack of which your gang will shoot you if they catch you at it. That's all. Just see where that lands you. And they won't try you too particularly. They may go through the forms of a trial, but they won't try you too particularly.

It's amusing, with us; we try anybody nowadays very much at ease. It's very charming. We're very much at ease, and so we just try 'em enough to drive 'em underground. The Russians try 'em enough to bury 'em underground. And there's a difference; a little difference!

To bring it round to what I wanted it all about, of course I've got to say one thing more. I've divided this world — (This is the chief thing I want to say.) — I've divided the world into two halves and given one half to the spiritual thing and one half to science. Now, I'm going to say one word more about science.

When I talk to scientists, I say to them: "Of course, all science is domestic science. It's just got to do with man's domestication on the planet or in the universe. No matter how far it reaches, it's got to do with our domestication."

And they say: "Oh, well, you mustn't say that. It goes higher than that. What are you going to say to the two-hundred-inch glass that is turned on the universe? Has that got anything to do with our domestication on the planet?"

"No! The trap is set, and you're caught. That's all I want you to say. The upper half of science, pure science, is as spiritual as anything else on this side."

There's half of spiritual, the upper half of science. And what is the name for it? "Curiosity"— the most spiritual thing man can have, just sheer, pure curiosity, disinterested curiosity. That's the upper half of science. And all I've left for gadgeteers and engineers is the lower right-hand corner.

Where poetry comes in

"Philosophy versus Wisdom" was the title of the Great Issues Course lecture given by Mr. Frost at Dartmouth on May 7, 1951, from which this excerpt has been taken. His incidental references to "talk right now down in Washington" and to "before any of this happened" relate to then-acute public concern for, as well as Congressional investigation of, criminal and corrupt practices both within and relating to the federal government.

I GET ASKED now and then, right out of a crowd, out of a forum or something — (I don't see many forums. This comes as near a forum as anything I face.) — but I get asked once in a while, "What philosophy has poetry, for a time like this?" You see, every commencement address begins like that: "In troubled times like this. . . ."

And of course the first thing to say about that, all times have been troubled, haven't they? I was looking at Matthew Arnold, and there's nothing but the trouble of that time through his poetry. You go back to Wordsworth, and he has a poem beginning:

> Milton! thou shouldst be living at this hour:
> England hath need of thee: she is a fen
> Of stagnant waters: . . .

You see, just like now.—

> . . . altar, sword, and pen . . .

That is, the church, literature, and the army; all corrupt, he says.—

15

Have forfeited their ancient English dower
Of inward happiness. . . .[10]

He thinks all the "inward"—which, again, is this thing that Shakespeare was talking about, the "inward happiness" part of it—he thought that was all gone: the inward happiness. And that's what some people think now.

Well, the answer is that I don't believe poetry has any philosophy for offer. To make a kind of poetic allegory or myth—Platonic sort of myth—let me put it this way: God sent into the world three things—just three, great things; the greatest things. Two of them were beliefs, and one of them was unbelief.

And one of the beliefs calls itself a "belief" and uses that word for itself all the time: true religion. (Though, it always has second breaths. It'll say, "Lord, I believe; help thou mine unbelief."[11] Unbelief goes with it, in true religion.) And the other belief, that doesn't always know it's only a belief, is science.

And the religion believes that you can't get human happiness in this world unless you think of an ultimate happiness in another world. And science believes—(It's a belief, too. Doesn't say so, but it ought to be reminded once in so often.)—it believes that some way or other, by piling up knowledge and going on from to know and to know and to know, that we can get human happiness here. [. . .]

I've named religion and science as the two great beliefs. And you can trace 'em, anytime you want to. You can look at 'em and just see what their value is.

And the third thing that God sent into the world, like a goddess or something, is the unbelief called "philosophy"—which is never its true self and never good when it isn't doubting, when it isn't pruning and trimming and combing the dead hair out of the two beliefs—like combing a dog, combing dogs.

Now, you look back. That sends your mind back over some

of the philosophers you know. They do — from their powerful position, of an almost all-powerful position — they try to help out the two beliefs now and then, when the poor things don't know what to say for themselves. They try to rationalize for 'em.

And the two beliefs themselves, when they get worried about the unbelief of philosophy, they become theologists. You'll find the religious people stealing from philosophy — stealing off into it, currying favor with philosophy, by becoming theologists. And you'll see the scientists doing the same thing — very much in our time; they've never done it so much as in our time. They've reached in and become Jeanses and Eddingtons. They've become what you call "sciologists," I guess.

Now, after I've said that and given you a chance to look it over, I wonder if you're wondering where I say poetry would come in. Well, it doesn't come in anywhere there. It doesn't match with those things at all.

It plays around over the surface of all those things, just the same as you do. You don't take any definite position in religion, and you don't take any definite position in science — though you're more in danger of doing that. And you don't adopt any one philosophy, any one skepticism.

See, all I think of in Socrates was the negative side. I heard a fine old man say the other day, "Well, I don't like you to use the words 'the negative side.'" Said, "I don't think it's nice to think about negative things."

But the negative is the cleansing. It's Socrates' demons that told him "no" and nothing else — never told him "yes" once; always told him "no." And that's what he was there for, to disturb the boys with "no," on the street corner — Alcibiades and the rest of 'em. That's why they gave him poison, in the end. The town couldn't stand him.

Now, poetry comes in like this. I don't want the word "phi-

17

losophy" for it at all; I don't. I want the word "wisdom"—little scraps of wisdom, little flashes of insight, just the same as you get every day among people.

You'll hear people say, "Once bit, twice shy." That's almost poetry, you see — the language is so queer, that use of "twice." "Once bit, twice shy." A lot to think about in that, a lot to think about. It doesn't say "twice" anything worse than "shy"—just "shy"; guarded the second time. It doesn't say "clear out," you know—just "shy."

We live with those things. We vote with 'em. We go to school with 'em. We play games with 'em. I'm not going to enumerate too many of them. Let me show you a few — and one or two in poetry, just to show you they're the same.

I often think a poem is nothing but a momentary stay against confusion. It's got something in it that's like that, that holds the moments for you, anyway — stops the confusion.

Now, take what I'm saying tonight about the three things God sent into the world — the three great ladies: two beliefs and one unbelief — to serve for the duration of the piece (p-i-e-c-e).

Somebody said I'm the champion exaggerator. Well, I'm not. I'm the honestest man there is. I never tell a lie. What I say there's always something to, anyway. Seems there's something to that.

I'll show you a deuce tonight for the fun of it, for your diversion: a couple of my own poems. I don't know whether poetry gets dragged in here or not. But she does tonight.

For years I've heard friends of mine, writers, say that we were to blame for the Revolution. The English weren't to blame at all, the British. We were to blame.

I knew someone who wrote that so successfully that the British would always lend him a battleship to go anywhere he pleased in. His name was [deliberately unintelligible mumble]. Can you hear me?

Then, I knew somebody else who said that all the best people — all the best people — pulled out of here when the Revolution began and went to live in Canada. And they're sitting up there in Canada talking about it at teatime now.

That's always bothered me a little. And I always hate the kind of the pettiness of that kind of thing. There's a largeness, there must be, beyond all that. And years ago I wrote a poem that must have been in answer to that, unconscious answer to that. It's a short poem in blank verse that I'm going to say to you, to show the kind of momentary stay against all the confusion that there is in that kind of talk.

There is today. Most of the talk right now down in Washington, that's going on, is very fine, very dignified. But there's a pettiness about the questions that are up. The main question is in danger of getting forgotten. It won't be. It'll emerge. Somebody'll keep it there, or between them they'll get to it in the end, after much pettiness of "You said this." and "No, I didn't say that; you said it." and "Were you awake at Wake Island?"

Well, sometime — after not getting too angry about all this confusion that you listen to — sometime a little clarification emerges. Years ago I wrote this, mind you. That's what I want you to notice: years ago. It's the history of the Revolutionary War. If I were to write a prose book, it would be no more than this, a whole book of prose on the history of the Revolutionary War. It virtually says this — (This makes it fit in with what's going on now, though I wrote it years ago.) — it's this: That war was the beginning of the end of colonialism. That's all it was.

No one was to blame on either side. 'Twas the beginning of the end of a great thing. Taught the British something; they took a hitch in their trousers and began over again, began to make it

19

better, so it'll last longer. And now you're seeing it, the end, going further, or everybody says that. [. . .]

[Mr. Frost said his poem "The Gift Outright."]

There's no whole philosophy in that, is there, unless it's implied? There's nothing more horrible to me than to have someone say I'm Platonic or Hegelian. I don't belong that way. That isn't where I am. I'm scatterbrained, that's all — bits of wisdom here and there, scraps of wisdom. [. . .]

> [Mr. Frost said his poem ultimately titled
> "America Is Hard to See," identifying it as "a
> rather recent one," and he commented on its
> line "On how to crowd but still be kind," say-
> ing: "You see, that's socialism. It's my latest on
> socialism. I'm always taking a new shot at it."]

Now, three or four other places in the course of my lifetime I've made a stab at socialism, in a kind of generous effort to understand it. I was brought up on Henry George and *Poverty and Progress*. An old family friend he was. And, so, I saw in capital letters very young — (In capital letters, way back; I don't know, back in the eighties or nineties sometime — in the eighties, I'd think.) — I saw for the first time the "HAVES" and the "HAVE NOTS" done in capital letters.

So, there it is, always in front of you. And what you going to say to it?

And look at it. Seems to come, come, come — come on, come on, you know — the socialism, in some form or other. There are all sorts of disguises for it — such as being taken care of by the state, being what some people call "stated."

Another place I say — just showing you how poetry has just little glimpses of it — another place I say [. . .] we'll all be "selfless foragers." I speak of "Our selfless forager Jerry"—Jerry being an ant I happen to know (a-n-t). "Our selfless forager Jerry."[12]

And another time, somewhere else —— Anymore I don't remember the words, but the idea goes like this: I've heard of the law of diminishing returns, and you've heard of it more than I have. But I pick a thing like that, the law of diminishing returns: Sure, yeah; maybe it's by the law of diminishing returns we arrive at socialism.

That's just another stab. It helps me for the moment. I sleep that night. [. . .]

Some people say we ought to get out of this by betting our bottom dollar. (That's Marshall Plan!) And then somebody else will point out — or ought to point out — that there's something deeper than that. We have that slang; we say, "I'll bet my bottom dollar." And there's another one: "You bet your sweet life."

And who'd win, the person that had bet his bottom dollar or the person that had bet his sweet life, if that's what it'd come to? It's forced on us — apparently, forced on us.

Well, that's all before any of this happened. But that's on my mind always. It comes, emerges in some little line. It isn't a whole philosophy and doesn't pretend to be. There's a certain amount of common wisdom in it.

It lies in those two slangs. Aren't they pretty ones: "You bet your bottom dollar" and "You bet your sweet life"? That's American philosophy versus Russian, right now. Ain't it hell to have to say so?

Handling figures of speech

In May of 1952 Mr. Frost traveled to Billings, Montana, to be the speaker at the high-school graduation of his grand-daughter Robin Fraser. While at Billings he also spoke at both Rocky Mountain College and the Eastern Montana College of Education. His May-eighteenth talk at the latter institution is represented by this excerpt, within which passing reference is made to U. S. Senator Estes Kefauver, who was then heading a highly publicized investigation of organized crime.

I WOULDN'T GO round the country advocating poetry or defending poetry or trying to make poetry out as of special value in education, I suppose. But I must think that it comes in somewhere, or I wouldn't be standing here, would I?

I think some of my friends in the educational world think that it is decorative, that it belongs to education as cloves belong to a ham. You stick the poetry into the ham, the solid education. And of course that isn't right. That wouldn't be the way to think of it at all.

It belongs to the very essence of it all, just as much as anything you can name, in its small way. It may not be in time; it may not take too much time in school. And I don't know how directly it ought to be taught. But from childhood up, it probably has its greatest value in preparing everybody in figures of speech, in metaphor.

And when you stop to think of it, all our wisdom, everything we know, is in figures of speech. When you look at the way people can go wrong about politics, religion, philosophy, it's from some misunderstanding of metaphor. Nearly everything that we say has a metaphorical basis.

For instance, I hear somebody say that "I'm a mechanist; that is, I believe the universe is a machine." He says he's a mechanist.

I'm finishing that for him. He leaves it that way: "I believe the world is a machine." And then I want to say to him: "That's a pretty good figure. What you're saying is, 'The world, the universe is *like unto* a machine.'" You see, "like unto."

And then I say: "If you're used to figures of speech, you must know that every figure of speech breaks down. You can only go a little way with it. It has a little significance and, then, it's gone; you have to have another figure of speech."

I say to him: "Now look, it's 'like unto a machine,' you say. Exactly 'like unto a machine'?" And I say: "All right, now, did you ever see a machine without a pedal for the foot, a button for the finger, or a lever for the hand? All those three things belong to a machine — all of them or one of them: pedal for the foot, button for the finger, a lever for the hand."

He says, "Yes."

"In the universe do you know where those are?"

"Well, then, I mean" — he says — "I mean it's like unto a machine, only it isn't like unto a machine."

He stayed too long with it.

From childhood up, there's always the intimation of something like that. And in the good poetry, beginning with Mother Goose, half the time you're asked to be on the lookout for some metaphor, some intimation of something else. It's as if you're saying, "Now I'm saying one thing, but while I'm saying that, I may be saying something more."

The double meaning. For instance, it says in Mother Goose, doesn't it?:

Pussy cat, pussy cat, where have you been? . . .

This is a famous poem, which I was brought up on.—

Pussy cat, pussy cat, where have you been? . . .

You see, it's an English poem. You can tell, because it says "been" to rhyme with "queen."—

. . . where have you been?

I've been to London to see the queen.
Pussy cat, pussy cat, what did you see there?
I saw . . .

Now, watch me make something else of it.—

I saw nothing but what I would have seen
    if I'd stayed at home.
I saw a little mouse run under a chair.

[. . .] Did that mean that to the child? No, but it got the child ready to play with that sort of thing, play with double meanings, ulteriorities.

Now, I'm inclined to think that half the trouble that they tell about in the world —— I don't believe that there are troubles any worse at any given time than 'tis at any other. If it is, I wouldn't be able to know it; I'm not smart enough.

I deplore the corruption today and agree that it's terrible, with Mr. Kefauver. But then I remember, as I look back — (I make a kind of figure.) — I say, "This time is like unto another time." That's what the history's about, making figures of speech like that.

As for corruption, in Athens the greatest man of all — the greatest statesman of all, that made Athens, for the short time it was the greatest thing in the world's history maybe, made it

24

that — named Pericles; he was tried for corruption and convicted. So, we meet it elsewhere, you see, corruption. (As someone said, sadly, "Things were never the same in Athens after that." Took the wind all out of it; Pericles lived afterward, but things weren't the same.)

But if there is anything wrong with our time — (And we are troubled about the thing.) — you know, I think that very often that it's nothing but an unpreparedness for the metaphors of Mr. Freud, for instance — as far as they go. Some metaphor about the child that has a little value in it, but you mustn't stay with it too long.

There are figures of speech, metaphors, that have more lasting value than others. But all of them, you learn — as you read poetry — you learn to know that you must leave 'em; love 'em and leave 'em. They have their beauty. It's insofar forth. That's all.

I ought to say that I've taught everything but the kindergarten myself. And all the way along, that's been a growing concern with me, about how we handle figures of speech, how to handle figures of speech. And that's what poetry is all about.

Some poems are almost without that ulteriority. But almost always there's a figure within the poem, scattered figures in details or a figure of the whole.

Now, of course, that's almost the same as saying that everything is allegorical. And 'tis. You've got five or six different names just for the metaphor: "allegory," "metaphor," and so on. You can't tell a story that anyone will listen to — no story has any valid interest — that hasn't got something of intimation. "Intimation" is another word for it. "Hinting" is another word for it. And how far the hint goes and where the hint stops, that's what we go into poetry to learn.

Now, that's only one of the things. That's the chief thing, though, in poetry — that to the mind, anyway; to the ear, something else. For instance, people are always looking for the *soundness* of poetry, whether it's genuinely *sound*, valid. That's all right, and that's an important thing — lies in the metaphor. And then the other thing is whether it's *a* sound, something to the ear.

I read poetry nowadays that seems to me not to have anything for my ear. It's as if the fellow that wrote it had had his own ears cut off, and he's content with the mental part of it, without the sound of it.

Now, I wanted chiefly to read to you tonight. That's what you're here to listen to. I'm not going to talk too long. Mind you, I haven't made too much of it.

You know, what I'd like to say of poetry: that it's some small part of that better half of the world that can't be made a science of. And when I say "better half," I say it partly as a good-humored jest — as we speak of our wives, you know, as our better halves. I just mean it's — somehow — it's a half.

And you might wonder about that, what I mean. But you can take whole poems. Take a poem of Shakespeare's. And he lists in one poem I can think of — (It's just like an itemized list of things that can't be made a science of. Over and over again the metaphor is the thing.) — he says:

> When in disgrace with fortune and men's eyes,
> I all alone beweep my outcast state,
> And trouble deaf heaven with my bootless cries . . .

You see, he's talking right away in a metaphorical way about prayer there: "trouble deaf heaven . . ." — (He's saying, for the moment he doesn't believe in prayer.) — "And trouble deaf heaven with my bootless cries." You see, heaven's deaf to me; he's saying that for the minute. He doesn't mean that's an unbelief entirely, except as he's speaking for him.—

26

> And trouble deaf heaven with my bootless cries,
> And look upon myself, and curse my fate,
> Wishing myself like one more rich in hope,
> Featur'd like him, like him with friends possess'd,
> Desiring this man's art, and that man's scope . . .

Take that as my concern. There are three or four other concerns there before you get to that. But when you get there, that's my concern as a writer: my scope and my art. I look on Whitman, for instance, and I can see that he decided to go in for scope, rather than art. And I look at another poet, like Landor, and I can see he decided to go in for art more than scope. But there it is, laid out for you in a grand figure, the pair of them there.—

> With what I most enjoy contented least . . .

You see, that's a figure of speech for the United States right now. All its writers are complaining — all but me. They're all complaining, though we've got everything in the world and everybody thinks we have everything in the world. But everybody's unhappy.—

> With what I most enjoy contented least;
> Yet in these thoughts myself almost despising . . .

Another grand figure for that thing in yourself that despises yourself.—

> Yet in these thoughts myself almost despising . . .

And then the whole thing a figure for what lifts you out of all this. He goes down, down, down, down, down, step by step — (That's the figure.) — and then he says:

> Haply I think on thee, — and then my state

(Like to the lark at break of day arising
From sullen earth) . . .

See, this is all the sullenness of earth.—

From sullen earth) sings hymns at heaven's gate. . . .[13]

And that's a figure — he makes that the figure — of love, you see; step after step. It's an itemized account, that is, of things that can't be made a science of. There's no science can touch any of that, never will.

We know how great science is; how remarkable 'tis; how wonderful, admirable, and all that, I'm saying. But there's a whole half of life that I live and you live that can't be touched with it.

And poetry always is insisting on that, in its figurative ways, always telling you what stays there: your concern that nobody can touch — psychology, psychiatry, and sociology; nothing that pretends to be science. "Haply I think on thee. . . ." See? Who is she? No science about it.

I rode in a car the other night with a young fellow who insisted that the happiest thing you could do in teaching was to rationalize for students a poem like that — (He didn't name that poem.) — but to rationalize it and show how defective it is.

I said, "You're one of these fellows that think you're better than anything you know what's the matter with."

All that is a kind of wisdom that goes with delight, too. There's a wisdom that's uncritical, somewhat uncritical.

He said, "You're irrational." I said: "Well, first of all there's delight, the delight of wisdom; and, then, the analysis of wisdom as you get older. But," I said, "you'll be too analytical by forty, anyway."

Well, I leave that there and go to these things, some of them, that I'll say to you. [. . .]

28

This first one I'll say to you is called "Birches." And this is in blank verse. Art and scope; some art and some scope. That's no boast. For years I didn't know that was my concern, about my art and my scope.

Landor says in a poem, "I strove with none, for none was worth my strife. . . ." Do you see what he was saying there? He was saying something that a whole administration of ours lived on. "I strove with none, for none was worth my strife. . . ." That's Wilson. He got that right out of that poem. President Wilson: "too proud to fight"; he translated it into "too proud to fight."—

> I strove with none, for none was worth my strife;
> Nature I loved . . .

And then this second line was what I wanted to get to:

> Nature I loved and, next to Nature, Art. . . .[14]

You see, he said "nature" for "scope." He thought he loved nature best, scope most. But he didn't. We tell him somebody else did. [. . .]

[Mr. Frost said his poem "Birches."]

One of the commonest, one of the deadliest figures of speech going: that you have to *leave* somewhere. There is such a thing as "escape." The other day a distinguished professor said to me, "Isn't poetry, on the whole, to be considered just an escape?" I said, "No, I always thought it was a pursuit."

That's just spoiling his figure, that's all. There is such a thing, but I said I didn't want to hear this figure of speech "escape" anymore. "Well," he said, "you're going to have to. It's all in criticism, all through everything, you know."

Why did you write poetry? Why do you whistle? Why do you sing? Is it an escape? No, it's a pursuit. I'm sure you're after something nice —*after* something. Nothing's after you but the devil!

"Anxiety for the Liberal Arts"

Here Mr. Frost's opening reference is to the title he had beforehand provided for his Great Issues Course lecture at Dartmouth on May 18, 1953. Midway of this excerpt he alludes whimsically, in an aside, to the college's Amos Tuck School of Business Administration.

I OUGHT NOT to have given out such a subject. I thought everybody was anxious about the liberal arts but me. I was going to make fun of everybody, but it seems nobody is anxious about 'em. I don't share this anxiety at all. I believe I must have got the idea from the president of some other college.

But there is something to be said about what may be coming to the liberal arts. I call 'em "the liberal arts," not just "the arts."

I can speak to you as just about to become alumni and owners of this college. You're not owners of it now. You may think you are, but you'll really be owners when you're alumni, won't you? You'll be electing trustees and regents and all that sort of thing, here and elsewhere maybe in the world.

And you'll have something to say the rest of your lives — maybe editorially on a paper or maybe reportorially, as slanting the news on some newspaper. But you'll be having something to say about the shape colleges are going to take.

Sometimes I wonder if the best colleges aren't going to be the private ones that own themselves, that don't belong to the government and can say what they want to be without consulting anybody in Washington. But I'm not sure of that. I'm not sure that in a great state university, the little liberal-arts college in the middle of it may not have a cozy place where it can do almost what it pleases, too — stay with the liberal arts and not get businesslike or too scientific or too anything but liberal arts.

Well, anyway, if I don't worry about the liberal arts, I can at least tell you what they are, can't I? And to do that, let me first tell you what you might expect me to know more about. Let me first tell you what poetry is.

The first thing that poetry is is both prose and verse. So I won't get into trouble there, let me say that at once. In the old days, in the old classical days, you'll find Cicero, though he wrote no verse at all, spoken of as a Roman poet. And I always in speaking of poetry, always mean prose and verse. Well, that's the first thing.

Let me tell you two or three things poetry is. Another thing is, I like to think, this. I've been where I had to talk about what was the nearest of kin to poetry in a college, what department was nearest of kin. Was it the English Department? No, I dismissed that. Was it the Philosophy Department? Was it this department? And then I came all the way down, and I decided that the nearest of kin was the athletic.

For what reason? Because poetry I regard as a kind of prowess, prowess in performance. It's performance. It isn't criticism. It isn't appreciation. It's performance. (I think the poetesses and the actresses and all the creative people in the world, they marry athletes. I'm always hearing that. Anyway, they ought to!)

I'm not going to linger too long on these details. I'm going to get to the main thing — by and by.

Now, another thing poetry is is to be put this way. I heard a lady speaking, a critic speaking, not so terribly long ago, and I heard her say, in a foreign accent, that the world is old, language is worn out, and there can be no more poetry.

And after she'd said that, I went up to her and I said — (I got up something to say to her.) — I said, "I thought poetry was the *renewal* of language." (A month or two after, I saw her writing an article to that effect, and she didn't give me credit at all!) It's the *renewal* of words. Good writing is the renewal of language.

And I might just say a word. It's the way words come in fresh, so that you say of them sometimes: "Well, I never saw that used just that way before. But, on second thought, it's very nice." That's what it is to write. That's what it is to make poetry, in prose or verse.

Then, another thing poetry is — (And I'm getting up higher with it all the time.) — it is the dawning — its got to have in it, anyway — it's the dawning on you of an idea; the freshness caught of an idea dawning on you.

Now, you must have had that experience. There's no more delight in the world than to be saying something, in a joke or an idea, just as it's coming on you; to be with the right people and have it that way.

Poetry has that freshness forever, of having caught the feeling that goes with an idea just as it comes over you.

You know it more familiarly in a joke or in a prank. A prank is like that. What's the fun of a prank if it's a studied prank? The mischief that comes over you is at its most delightful just as it comes over you, while you're up to it.

Now, that belongs to poetry. That's another thing. And if you never knew what that was, you don't know what I'm talking about — if you never tasted that experience. And, between you and me, it's all I hang around poetry for, to have that happen to me — that I'm just right when I'm right where I can catch what's coming over me, in verse. (Me with verse, not prose; I'm more interested in it that way.)

But I have the same feeling with people, of an evening when four or five things have come over me like mischief, as we talked, you know—all that pleasure, that freshness; the freshness of dawn.

And then the greatest thing of all, I suppose, is that poetry, in prose and verse, is always the free field of metaphor, for those that are good at making it and for those that are good at taking it.

When I say, "I'd like to 'put it across' tonight," I'd be sorry if all you boys weren't in on that metaphor: "put it across." I'd be sorry if most girls weren't. I hope they get taken to baseball games, too, some.

When I say, "I wouldn't mind, you know, with some people, 'putting one over on him.'" You see, that's different, isn't it? "Putting it across"; and the other's "put one over on him," so he got a strike called.

Now, we live—outside and inside of school—we live in the metaphor, the symbol. [. . .]

I'm going to say a little poetry to you tonight, ring in a few of my poems. But let me try one, a strange one to you—ask you to strain a little. Sometimes you have to strain about these things.

Suppose I said to you that a great nation isn't a progression from another great nation that went before it. There's no progress to be seen in that. The great nation has a beginning and a middle and an end. And then there's another great nation has a beginning and a middle and an end. It's more like the phoenix than anything else.

This isn't a class and I can't ask you to raise your hands, but I bet a lot of you aren't in on that. And I don't know that you ought to be.

Many a figure, many a metaphor, many a symbol you have to take the context—there has to be some context with—and you can do it. And I'm against its having to need any footnotes. I don't see any fun to that.

The fun is the free field of metaphor that I'm some good in

and you're some good in. And you don't have to be let in on it. You don't have to be taken off and be "brainwashed" about it. (There's another figure, you see — fresh one, very fresh. It's not one of my making.)

I've written a book of six hundred pages, and it's all full of metaphors of *my* making, but I take it you follow — that most people can follow — without any footnotes.

But, now, the phoenix is a bird that doesn't lay an egg. That's one thing about it. It begins, lives to a peak, and dies in a fire — in a blaze of fire. And out of the fire rises the next bird, the next phoenix. And there's only one in the world at a time — just the same as there's only one great nation in the world at a time. That's what I'm saying.

The birth of a nation is like that. It rises, you know, big from something else, but not derived in the way of birth — rises out of the ashes.

Now, maybe you'd be amused to struggle with a poem about the phoenix, to show what it is. Let's see if I can remember that; not mine:

> By feathers green, across Casbeen . . .

Can you do that "Casbeen"? You see, it's a word a little different from the one you know that by, isn't it? But it's an older form of it. Just the same as if I said "Hi·mal′·a·yas" to you, you'd know I meant the "Him·a·lay′·as." It's just as easy as that.—

> By feathers green, across Casbeen
>   The travellers tracked the Phoenix flown,
> By gems he strew'd in waste and wood,
>   And jewell'd plumes at random thrown:
>
> Till wandering far, by the moon and star,
>   They stand beside the fruitful pyre,

Where bursting bright with sanguine light
   The impulsive bird forgets his sire.

You see, it all lies to that:

Where bursting bright with sanguine light
   The impulsive bird forgets his sire.

It's a way of speaking. You know, poetry's always a way of speaking. And can you take it?—

Those ashes shine like ruby wine,
   Like bag of Tyrian murex spilt,
The claws, the jowl of the flying fowl
   Are with the glorious anguish gilt.

It's an anguishing affair, you see.—

. . . with the glorious anguish gilt.

So rare the sight . . .

Not many have seen it; I never have.—

So rare the sight, so rich the light,
   Those pilgrim men, on profit bent . . .

From the Tuck School!—

Those pilgrim men, on profit bent,
Drop hands and eyes and merchandise,
   And are with gazing most content.[15]

You see, I didn't help you any with that. You did it yourself! Now, I'll try another one with you.

Suppose I say a poem of mine and tell you how people have made a figure out of it, and then tell you what I make out of it.

I can do that, too. Others do it to my poems. I do it to other people's poems. And I do it to my own — when I have to.

This one goes like this. It's called "Mending Wall." This ought to be part of your education. I don't want it to be so much a part of your education that it's been staled to you. You see, I always dread that. (Always drawing parallels, you are. Poor Longfellow perished, almost, of being used too much in school. Spare me!)

Well, here's the poem. [. . .]

[Mr. Frost said his poem "Mending Wall."]

You may have heard, some of you, that that's been turned into a poem about nationalism and internationalism. "Something there is that doesn't love a wall" is the international, you see. They could say that if they want to. And "Good fences make good neighbors" is nationalist. And then I have to defend myself and go 'em one better about it.

You don't know what I'll do with it. I say: "Those two are one man talking both ways, man the wall-builder and wall-upsetter, the boundary-maker and the boundary-breaker. You see, it's two men, but they're one." (I got this up afterward, after the fact.)

Then, I say this, that "That's just what man is, outside himself and inside himself." While I'm talking to you here, my cell walls are breaking down and making at the same time. That's what I exist by, cell walls going down and cell walls coming up and forming again, reforming. That's life. And so I say that life is cellular, both within and without. (Even the communists have cells!)

Well, I say that all to illustrate that part of the thing. Kipling has a poem that goes:

> In the days of old Rameses,
> That story had pareses,
> Are you on—are you on—are you on?[16]

36

We're always saying — in every poem we say, every remark we make — we're saying in a pathetic, pleading way "are you on"; do you get it? We don't cry about it. But that's what we're doing.

Take Mr. Einstein, the great scientist. (You see, you think this all just belongs to poetry.) Years ago somebody said for Einstein — (I don't believe he said it himself.) — there were only twelve people in the world could understand what he was talking about. And since then he's written several books. He's come out of his mathematics into just the liberal arts, the poetry of language, to try to tell us what he does mean.

And on his birthday, he gave us two interesting figures of speech, metaphors. He said he wasn't sure, after all, that he'd got away on the right assumption, in all his thinking. He wasn't sure — he didn't know for sure — whether the universe was made of "jelly" or of "sand." Now, that goes way back to Greek philosophers, those two metaphors: jelly or sand.

Then, he said another one. He said, "Here I'm asked to describe the universe ——" (Nobody asked him but himself. But, as a matter of fact, he said that.) "Here I'm asked to describe the universe, and all I've got to make it out of is a couple of bones — or as if I'd just been given a couple of bones to describe a megatherium." Poor man!

But the eagerness, the eagerness we have to understand each other is always coming out in metaphor, symbol — nowhere else. As I like to say once in a while, "I make bold to say" that there's no such thing as thought — you've never had a thought — unless you've made a metaphor, an analogy, an allegory. You've never had a thought. You've had opinions. But what I call "thought" begins with connecting things in metaphor.

I use the word all down the line: "metaphor," "simile," "analogy," "allegory," "parable." [. . .]

Now, I've said up to this point what poetry is. The best thing of all, it's this free field of metaphorical action, play, where you disport yourself — for that is thought and that alone is thought; almost alone, almost alone that is thought.

Then, the last thing to say is that poetry — (And this is intended to offend you. I hope it offends a few.) — poetry *is* the liberal arts. It's the whole business, poetry in prose and verse.

Let me say one more thing that poetry is. Poetry is that that evaporates from both prose and verse when it's translated. All this translated stuff around is short of being poetry. It's lost its poetry in being translated.

You can see what I mean by the liberal arts. In showing you a little about that, suppose I say what is poetry in history. Is it the hundred best books? Ninety of 'em are in translation, so they're out. There they go; bang! What other, then? [. . .]

Well, we've got in our own language English historians and American historians that I hold up at that place. They're not textbooks enough; they're not used as textbooks enough. Think of the names. There's Gibbon; there's Macaulay; there's Froude. Come over here, there's Parkman; there's Prescott.

You know, there's enough for a course in history, right there, without going to these darned translations. You've got Gibbon forever. I never have Gibbon far away from me.

That's what I mean. That's the liberal arts in history.

Little more to say? Let me show you in somebody else's poetry a couple of things before I leave it. I said that phoenix one to you. I used that phoenix as a symbol of nations rising from nations, leaping from the destruction of nations. That's my idea of the way nations come; one in the world at a time, practically.

Then, suppose I just let you look at a couple of things. What do you make of this? There's a poem by a friend of mine that's called "The Hollow Man." Get that? (Another figure like that we have. I wonder if he doesn't mean "stuffed shirt"? You see, that's another figure. But the hollow man's all right; another kind of figure.) He has these lines in it. He has the hollow men dancing around a "prickly pear." (pär — I must pronounce it right. I'm not from St. Louis!) They're saying:

> Here we go round the prickly pear
> The prickly pear the prickly pear. . . .

You see, like that. And you get that — desert; "prickly pear"? You see just what he must mean by all that. That's as easy as rolling off a log.

(You can often get these figures wrong. I used to think "rolling off a log" meant lying on a log and rolling off of it yourself. But it means rolling it off at the skidway. I see that now; matured, I have.)

You want to be left to yourself about 'em and get a chance to think 'em out. You don't want somebody to tell you. "Don't tell me," I always think, you know, when somebody tries to tell me everything. "Don't tell me; let me alone; mind your own business."

Here's one I didn't puzzle over. I was wrong with it for years. It's this one. Keats wanted to have it said of him that his name was "writ in water."[17] And, you see, what I had, I had a vision of his name being writ on a pond, written on a pond or on a river or on the ocean or something.

He didn't mean that. He meant with a pen dipped in water. (The same as you'd say — if I was Hitler or somebody — my name was "writ in blood.") My name was writ in ink; my name was writ in water. He means his pen dipped in water. (It'd been nice if his name had been dipped in lemon juice, wouldn't it? Because that would come out later!)

You see, all this fooling is — this is the whole business. I'm throwing 'em around with you.

Then, T. S. Eliot winds up that poem about "Here we go round the prickly pear / The prickly pear . . . ," he winds it up with this:

> This is the way the world ends . . .

Haven't you heard it? With his fine voice, he does it beautifully. It's one of the best things to listen to.—

> This is the way the world ends . . .

He has to say that three times.—

> This is the way the world ends
> Not with a bang but a whimper.

Two figures there. He prefers the second one, he says. He can be completely wrong about that, you know. I haven't seen it end yet. And I don't think it's ending with a bang. And I'm sure it isn't ending with a whimper. There are a few people whimpering. They're another "lost generation," I suppose. You've always got some generation getting lost.

Well, now look, somebody else says that "There is no past, there is no future, all is the present."[18] Now, you can say that like a philistine — (If you know what that figure is. It's another figure.) — you can say that like a coarse, common fool. There's only the present and my bread and butter.

No. The liberal arts are for the purpose of giving you a very extensive present; I agree to the present. The question with you when you're old — you know, and counting your score — the question is, "What has been the extent of my present; how wide and how long, backward and forward?"

You can't stretch it very far forward. We do our best to stretch it forward, with our dreams and our "ideals," as we call 'em. But the stretch back is a very important thing. [. . .]

40

So, the liberal arts are poetry, in my double sense of the word. And that means a very extensive thing. I bring in Einstein. I bring in Egypt. I bring in all I can for breadth and length, in my education. But it all centers in: "Words alone are a certain good"[19] — some poet says. That's the liberal arts.

When you get into a graduate school there's something else. There are specialities coming and all that. That's just what I leave out. But this is the length and breadth, the extent of your present. You don't want a stupid, nose-in-the-ground present.

Einstein says the universe is limited and that it's curved. And then I like to say, for the fun of it: "I know why he thinks the universe is curved. Because all reasoning is in a circle. And all reasoning is in a circle because of the shape of the brain pan."

That's my interference with these things. But I'm playing this just the same as he is and the same as you are. I can do it and I can take it. That's the thing. [. . .]

The whole poetry of poetry is like this. This cultivation is to get people so — in a family, we'll say; when they're grown up and have a family and everybody's living together — so when one hints, the others don't miss the hint. And when one doesn't hint, nobody takes a hint.

See, get it right. And when nobody's got a double meaning, to know that nobody has a double meaning. But when a double meaning — where there's an intimation of something else — to get it.

See, that's what the liberal arts are. And that's living every day, all the time. It isn't just in school. It's been going on with you for years.

I could string out a lot of baseball ones or football ones and all sorts of business ones. It's very important to be — *all* important — to be good at metaphor and intimations and hints and all these things — double entendres, you know.

A book side to everything

Having lectured the previous evening to Dartmouth seniors in the Great Issues Course, Mr. Frost met the following
morning with those students for a follow-up discussion
session. Then, on the afternoon of that same day, May 19,
1953, he both talked and recited selections of his own
poetry to undergraduates enrolled in the college's first-
year English classes, concentrating his remarks on the subject of books and reading.

SOMEBODY SAID to me — man well along in years, not a young
man, anyway; lawyer in New York and a very cultivated man — he
asked me if I took this magazine and that magazine and so on. I
said, "No." He said, "Don't you read any reviews?" I said, "No."
He said, "How do you know what to read?" I said, "Oh, I kind of,
you know — I pick it out of the air."

(I'll review books without reading them — never in writing,
always in conversation. You hear me talk about a book, and
somebody that I know will say, "You haven't read that." — under
their breath. And I say, "Shut up!")

He said to me, "You've *got* to read, haven't you?" I said,
"Yeah." I said, "But what have you *got* to read?" (You know the
expression "you *gotta* live." He said it like that, almost: "you *gotta*
read.") I said, "What have you *gotta* read?"

And it seems to me that's an interesting question. What
have you gotta read?

I've always sympathized with people who had four years of
education where they had to read more books a year than I've
read in a lifetime. And that's no exaggeration. I've watched my

granddaughters reading more books a week than I'd read in ten years. They look kind of jaded, and I hate to see girls look that way. (I'd rather see boys look jaded than girls!)

Well, I've thought of a way out of it all. I have said that the reason for coming to college is to learn how to read, in case you didn't learn in the high school. If you learned to read in the high school, the same as I did, you didn't have to go to college. [. . .]

But what is all this book business, this crowded book business, in college? I'll tell you. You're not reading these books, you're *scanning* 'em to see which ones of 'em you're going to live with the rest of your life. That's all it is — (You can't call it "reading," what you do. The quantity of it is too much to be called "reading," from my point of view.) — scanning the books to see which ones of 'em you'll want to live with the rest of your life.

I long since got so I don't go to a library. I can't live without certain books within reach of me, and I have to own 'em; can't go to a library for 'em.

I've been talking about figures this morning to seniors — the other end of whatever it is; the agony. And this is the way I think of books. I have taken into my play, my mental play — one way and another, hook and crook, hearing about 'em, scanning 'em in school, and all that — I've taken into play a certain number of books. It's quite a number. And I've got to have 'em in my head, mostly — but within my reach to renew 'em in my head whenever I feel they're getting out of mental play, so they don't come to me right.

And it reminds me of what I saw on the stage once. You've seen something like what I mean. I don't believe you ever saw as elaborate a one as I saw. You've seen a juggler playing three balls in the air; four balls in the air; five balls in the air; six balls in the air — and keep 'em all going, all floating between his two hands.

Now, I've seen something more elaborate than that. I saw a

man stand on a stage like this, and somebody behind him threw him — "scaled him," as we say (You know the expression?) — he scaled him a straw hat, wrong side up, with a stiff brim. And he took it on his finger and spun it, like this. And then they threw him another one, and he spun that on that hand. Then he began to fill the air with hat after hat. He took 'em, and he had 'em floating and coming and going. The whole theatre was full of his hats. And he never dropped one.

He had no more hats than he could keep in play. And someday you'll reach that point with the books. You'll add a little bit to it as your interests widen.

I have this weakness about it. If I go away for any length of time, I'm distressed at leaving all my books out of my reach. And I've taken, sometimes, with me more than I needed — the ones that I'm most apt to want a sentence from or the name of somebody from or an idea from. And I could name you those books. They're not the hundred best books. But they're some of the best books in the world, just the same.

I've been showing my prejudice too much to books that are in translation. Almost none of these are translated — (They're almost always in the English language.) — that I depend on that way. And I don't have to touch 'em too often. Once in a while I feel one growing dim to me, and I want it more in play, more where I can command it.

And how do I want to command it? In the many associations of life — (Associations; they come up.) — quite a good many of 'em, all things considered, considering who I am. But that's with me.

My mind isn't a card case, and I don't live in a card case. There's a free play of men and books. And the excuse I make for all this hard reading in school is that you're merely scanning 'em. (You wouldn't be able to stand what I call my kind of an examination in them, and you're not expected to be.) They're the books you're going to live with. You'll select among 'em.

Now, some of you won't do any of that, and that'll be your own good-bad loss, that's all. One thing you come to college for — one thing you get educated for — is to learn that there's a book side to everything, a book side.

You can get along without its book side. But the difference between you and people that haven't ever been with books — and been sort of baptized in books — the difference is that you always, whatever you're doing, you'll be thinking: "Well, what's the book? Where's the book about this? What's the book? There must be a book side to it; and I can find it."

That's all I want to say: book side to everything. And I've been surprised at the educated people I've known who hadn't that in their nature.

I've had the amusing fortune to have lived in a good many sabbatical houses. I've been at colleges where somebody was away on a sabbatical, and I was there, a visiting professor or something, a lecturer; and I had a sabbatical house. I saw the inside of a good many minds that way.

And I've been surprised to be in the house of some old professor without any books, except on the parlor table — one or two gift books, you know; they got 'em for Christmas. And that's the extent of it.

And then I've lived with the other extreme. I lived in a beautiful old, old house in Ann Arbor. I'll never forget it. (We almost lost it by fire — not my fault, but the next house to us.) The whole house — every room in it, every bedroom, everything — was just simply covered with books.

The funny part of it was — ('Twas an old scholar that lived there. His widow rented the house, let the house to us. She went off to Washington to listen to the Senators, and we had the house.) — every book I ever opened there, every single book, had had its spelling and punctuation corrected; every one I opened. [. . .]

But that was another kind of bookishness. That's extreme. Then, the other extreme of no books at all. And I knew an old lady who always dismissed koine, the common man, as having been brought up in a "bookless home." She always said, "He'd, poor man, been brought up in a bookless home."

That's what we're talking about. Who's bookless? And who's partly booked? And who is booked enough? And who's booked too much, maybe? [. . .]

Then, I want to say just one thing more to you. One of the things that interests me most in life is how soon eyes find eyes. An infant, you know, finds eyes. Eyes find eyes, and eyes stay with eyes all our lives. And I've got a poem that begins like this:

> Eyes seeking the response of eyes . . .

You see, that's the depth of all our feeling. —

> Eyes seeking the response of eyes . . .

It begins that way. I shan't go far with it. But just a little of it is like this:

> Eyes seeking the response of eyes . . .

So hungry for eyes—

> Bring out the stars, bring out the flowers,
> Thus concentrating earth and skies . . .

Our longing for eyes brings out the stars, brings out the flowers. That's where they came from.—

> Thus concentrating earth and skies . . .

46

You see. Why do we want to concentrate that great rubbish heap, the earth and sky? It's a great rubbish heap. We have to concentrate it—

So none need be afraid of size. . . .[20]

That's what the poem is. I was thinking of that as I watched you. What am I doing here? Seeking the response of eyes. You're not speaking to me at all. But I see a good many — don't stay with any.

It's a strange thing about we seek the eyes, but they're almost as blinding to look at as the sun is. Isn't that funny? We kind of keep easing off them, looking at 'em.

—at the dedication of a new wing of
Choate School's Mellon Library, May 5, 1962:

THIS is a book occasion, and I'm a book person from the word "go."

I've wanted [. . .] not to be a "book fool." (You know, that's one of our country sayings: "He's a book fool.") I wanted not to be a book fool, but at the risk of being a book fool, I've been a bookman — lived with the books. [. . .]

I remember when it dawned on me that I liked to think that you couldn't put a page of anything in front of me that I'd miss any tricks in. I always liked to think I could size up a page and that that was all of life to me — that I could size up a page; they couldn't hide anything from me. That's been my life.

Not freedom from, but freedom of

This text is drawn from Mr. Frost's May 17, 1954, Great Issues Course lecture at Dartmouth College.

WHAT AM I thinking about now, at eighty? Well, I'll tell you what I'm thinking about. I'm thinking about freedom a good deal. I can't have lived with all these free-verse writers that you read, without having considered the matter of freedom.

Freedom from what? Why are they called "free-verse writers"? (At one of their picnic parties, I guess 'twas, there was a sign up — a little box with some poems in the box — and it said "FREE VERSE HELP YOURSELF.")

But free verse, what is it free *from* — from?

What's the other preposition? (Of course the business of going to college, sometimes it seems to me, is all a matter of learning prepositions, getting you discriminating with prepositions.) Down in New York, for instance, all my friends love to think they have the freedom *of* the city.

That's why they're there, seven million of them. (How many is it?) They're there because they think they have achieved the freedom of the city — its theatres, its streets, its everything, you know; all its advantages. But for their children, they want freedom *from* the city. So, they take them out to raise 'em in Connecticut.

Now, there's the two: the *of* and *from* — freedom from. And the free-verse writer has taken the freedom *from* rhyme and metre. I'm not disparaging him when I say that, but that's what he's wanted, freedom from rhyme and metre, because he thinks

48

he's less likely to be sincere and sociological, and do the world less good, you see. He can say what he means, and he can talk deeper and darker and more earnestly, if he isn't bothered with the frivolity of rhyme and metre. That's the doctrine.

Well, that's all right. One wouldn't quarrel with that. I read somewhere that when I talked a little this way not so many days ago that I "attacked" free verse. But that's no attack on free verse. That's praising free verse for its attempt to be more sincere than any other kind of verse — get down to things. And they'll say, "Well, there are grave subjects, aren't there, that you wouldn't want to be rhyming about or writing metre about?"

The only defense for that would be — or one defense for doing the other thing; writing metre, anyway — would be Shakespeare. He writes about King Lear — (And that's about as deep and dark and serious as anything can be.) — and he calls it a "play." He's just playing, when he writes it. He does it in metre, plays it in metre; plays it very well, as you know.

Well, let's begin. I begin with the dictionary. If I were revolutionary enough, I might say I'm going to get along without the dictionary; I'm going to get free from the dictionary — and write *Finnegans Wake*. All right, if you want to take that chance. It's an awful chance to take. There aren't many'll follow you.

The freest way would be to get rid of words entirely and simply scream. If you got your true feeling, you'll say, "That's the way I feel ——" Scream like a siren, up and down.

Then, there's another freedom I want — not freedom *from*, but freedom *of*. I want the freedom of our syntax and our idiom; the idiom particularly. I'd like to command — command the dictionary; command the idiom more than anything else. I'd rather have all the uses of "the," the article "the" — the six or seven uses of it that I could think of — than to have seven different words; the idiomatic.

I've always thought that. I remember lecturing on that about twenty years ago, that subject, with John Erskine present. 'Twas a meeting of vocabularians. They were all there to talk about vocabulary. And I talked anti-vocabulary. I talked idiom. I had to, you know. Had to have some opposition, they had to have.

The freedom, then, of the dictionary, the freedom of idiom; and then one more freedom, that I didn't need to achieve or attempt, was the freedom of rhyme and metre. You see, could I swing the dictionary, swing the idiom, and swing the rhyme and metre? That was sort of excessive. That was from an exuberance of spirit.

It's the same about your country. It's the same about a ball field. It's the same about a tennis court. You don't want a freedom *from* the tennis court, you want the freedom *of* the tennis court, with the net just so high and the court just so large, always. And you don't want to go to conventions for changing the tennis court, like reformers. You're no reformer, you just want to see what good you are on the tennis court as is.

And so I — with these things — I accept the dictionary; I accept the idiom; I accept the rhyme and metre. But beyond all that is a love of a hope that I have won the freedom of my own country, that I can say almost anything anywhere in it and not be in bad taste.

Somebody, a friend of mine — oh, a very distant friend of mine, who writes verse; regular verse, not free — lately put on a record — for use in the United States generally — put on a record along with some others. And he thought he must assert this other kind of freedom. He must break down the rules. So, he got his money in advance, and then he stipulated that nothing should be altered, and then he put on a lot of dirty words.

And then he said, "Well, that's in all the books, you know, *From Here to Eternity* and everywhere else." And why hadn't he a right to put 'em on the air? And now that's going on; it's being settled.

A lot of people say that's freedom of speech. And what is that line? Well, now, I wouldn't be bothered with anything like that. I'm not interested in freedom *from* any particular rules. I'm interested in my own freedom *of* things.

Freedom of the city. Someone gave me the key to the city of Gloucester a little while ago. So, I have the freedom of Gloucester, anyway, if I haven't of New York. I can do anything I please there, within the law. I haven't got the key with me, but I've got it, a little gold key, a nice one. ("Keys" is the word usually. Plural is the way we say that: "the keys to the city." I should have had more than one, but I've only got one — symbol.)

Now, what's beyond it all? What freedom am I thinking of more than all?

There ought to be something done in psychology, some rule of thumb, that would help us free, so that we could get from an attachment to an attraction — change countries, for instance, change loyalties. There's an old poem that says:

> All those who change old loves for new
> Pray gods they change for worse![21]

Well, there ought to be some help about that. How do you get from loving one person to loving another? Or how do you get from loving one country to loving another? How do you change loyalties? [. . .]

What are the limitations of psychology? Can psychology help us? Put that down in your mind, will you, for me? Is there any psychology to help you about getting from an attachment to an attraction?

That isn't of interest to me, how you escape. That's the escape idea. How do you escape? Is freedom escape?

No, freedom isn't escape at all, for me. You see, you'd think that a life was an escape from an escape from an escape from an escape. And so you went on until you got buried, escaping something all the time, with drink and everything.

I'd rather if anybody was going to drink it wouldn't be for escape. I'd do it as a pursuit. There's a certain pride in that, isn't there; a pride in doing things in your life being a pursuit not an escape?

I loathe the word "escape." It's that other thing: *from* always. And pursuit *of* and freedom *of* — skill, ability; in the court as it is, in the form of society as it is.

And then I'm going to not make it too much longer; just one thing more to say. The freedom *of* my material is what makes me a thinker, if I am one — freedom *of* my material.

A schoolboy, by definition, is somebody who can tell you what he's learned, in the order in which he learned it. And a free person is a person who's forgotten more than most people will ever know. He's let it all scatter out and break down in his mind. And he can bring it together in his own forms by his own power of association.

And the whole of writing, of course, is that. All of having an idea is bringing things together that people hadn't brought together before, that bring freshness to the conversations, associations.

Your free associations are a proof that you have the freedom of your material you take out of different levels of knowledge, different times in your life — out of school, out of books, out of play, out of the past, out of the present, out of dreams — everything.

And things come together in pair. Things pair with a kind of love of each other. Things pair, and that's what makes poems. That's what makes metaphor. That's what makes thinking; makes everything.

When Schopenhauer said *The World as Will* . . . , all he was saying was a vast metaphor: that the universe or the whole thing may be likened unto that quality in man which we call "will." That's all he was saying. And it hadn't been said before. 'Twas one of those great things, that he must have felt strangely free in — that he'd commanded those two things that hadn't been together before.

And I suppose if we're here for any reason at all, it's to get more and more of that freedom, the freedom of association.

I don't think anybody's thought at all unless he's surprised himself and surprised other people, now and then, by putting two unexpected things together — unexpected by him; surprise a little to him, as well. No surprise in him, no surprise in his listeners. He's got to be a little surprised and pleased, so they'll be surprised and pleased.

The freedom that you can put it all into, it's all yourself. I wonder what gives you it. You have all the stuff, all the material of the years, all broken down and scattered in your mind in a beautiful disorder. And you can say, if you think about it, how chaotic it all is. But how delightfully chaotic. You're the boy what can put order into it, gleams of order, with associations like that.

When people talk about being confused, it's because they're contemplating all they know, without the ability to do anything with it. Any little thing gives you the sense of power, any little combination you make. And the more unexpected to yourself and to others, of course, the happier, the more felicitous.

I wonder when I have it most. I always think it's from well-being. I have to feel fine from having been outdoors and had a good time or been with nice people — and in being in a nice frame of mind, not being able to remember any of my enemies. If a thought of some enemy crosses my mind, that's apt to spoil this happiness of command.

It's the one self-assertion; it's the top assertion: the giving a little bit of form to what looks all chaotic and disorderly. And it's all yours or it's nothing.

You're just now, most of you — most of you are just getting some more material. And the question is, can you command it or do you want to command it in the sense in which I say? It isn't for literary men just. It's for thinkers. It's for inventors. It's for scientists.

The simple thing that we know Fermi for; we know him for having thought of the thing which we were all surprised that he should think of — very simple. You'd think that one particle of matter would be more apt to break into another one if it was going fast, charging hard, wouldn't you? It occurred to him to try it to see if slowing it up wouldn't do it. And it did it. And that's what the whole business is.

That's one. And his name, you see, one of the greatest names of our time. A little thought like that.

And so, then, in the end the one freedom we ask for is the freedom of the city, the freedom of our own material, the freedom of the books, the freedom — you might say — freedom of the city of life. And it doesn't very much matter about freedom of speech. (There were "Four Freedoms" they used to talk about then, and they were a funny assortment.)

This is a central freedom: the freedom of your own material. That's all there is to mind.

If you don't get it here and enter into it here, you can enter into it outside. We were saying, some of us, the other day that man is either self-made in college or self-made out of college. It's what you mean by "self-made" — passing that threshold into that sense of responsibility to do something with the disordered material that has been supplied you by the confusion of the order and disorder, the broken-down order and everything of life.

Of rapid reading and
what we call "completion"

This excerpt, from an appearance before a community audience in Hanover, New Hampshire, on December 15, 1954, contains reminiscences of Robert Frost's own undergraduate days at Dartmouth, as well as brief references to two Dartmouth friends, Henry C. Morrison, New Hampshire's Superintendent of Public Instruction, 1904–17, and John Sloan Dickey, the President of the College, who was on the platform with Mr. Frost to introduce him on this occasion.

I GO BACK to memories in New Hampshire of a great stir there was — in, oh, the early part of this century — in the educational world among teachers under Henry Morrison (a Dartmouth man, then State Superintendent) about "rapid reading." And I'm hearing the swan song of the rapid-reading people now, in the educational world.

I've just been seeing somebody who says we're busy now disabusing everybody of the idea of rapid reading. Fifty years that makes, just about — a little less than fifty years — cycle like that. And I've lived through it all. I didn't like it anytime, because I was never a rapid reader. I'm glad it's over.

The fact is I've been reading slower and slower, and I had to say something on my side about it. And I said what I still would hold. (You say many good things in self-defense, and you needn't be ashamed of 'em simply because they're in self-defense, you know. People may say, "Oh, you just say that!" Well, you do "just say that.")

And my defense was this: that anyone who is used to poetry can't read any faster than he hears it. And if he doesn't read much poetry, and forms the kind of skipping-eye sort of reading, that's all right. I don't know too much to say against that, though there's something. But the great thing is that: that if you read, prose and verse, to the speed of the ear, you've got to be a slow reader.

And the custom of reading verse will establish a habit of slow reading, as if it were spoken, though you don't move your lips. And of course poetry, and prose that is as good as poetry, must be read that way.

No one who ever writes good prose or verse but will write to the reading ear. That's what makes the essayist. That's what makes a person stand out among editorial writers, like E. B. White — with that to the ear.

One doesn't have to labor that too much. But the thing I thought I'd speak of tonight was ideas of poetry, like that. I haven't thought of that for quite a while. But every little while I think of something that arises from my interest in poetry.

That's very sound. Some of them are sort of wickedly unsound. I like to be that way sometimes. I can't help liking to be that way. There's so little chance left for rebellion in the world — unless we have a great rebellion. Little rebellions: the liberties I take, not the liberty that's given me; the liberties I take. [. . .]

Just let me say, too, in passing, that it's interesting to me about poetry and Dartmouth and New Hampshire and those first days of my interest in it all, early in my days of interest in it all. The next year after I ran away from here, I was in print in one of the better magazines. I was already started on this poetic career. And I've often told it around here — probably never as publicly as this — that the literary magazine that I sent my first poem out to, took my first poem out, and that it was a magazine I got acquainted with on the newspaper rack in the old library here.

I didn't know where to send things. I didn't go to summer schools where they teach people where to send their manuscripts. I didn't know how to make a manuscript out. And, in fact, when the little check came for the poem and a little note asking me who I was and so on, they asked me to spell the name of the magazine correctly next time I wrote to them.

You can guess the way I may have misspelled it. (I still misspell words, I notice; people say I do.) The magazine was known as *The Independent*. You can guess what I did to that, maybe.

I can remember in that poem the first sense I had of the nicety of the words — that nobody else — that I couldn't myself say differently. That is to say, I couldn't translate it even into other English. It's the same thing.

If I know anything about writing, or about reading either, it's that if you have an idea so complete that it's already in phrases and everything — partly in phrases — you are in danger of being a translator when you write. [. . .]

If you had the idea and wrote it out in prose, it's done. You can't turn it into a poem. That would be a translation, from English into other English.

And that's all very, very close to the truth. That's being too fastidious, you think; being precious? No; no.

When I have an idea a long time before I get to writing, it can reach a point when I'm aware of its being too much done to be made into a poem. (So, I use it for a lecture!) It's past the point; too well-done.

And that's very, very true. A whole lot of my life I've been so kind of idly busy — around, you know — that many a time I wasn't where I could have dealt with a poem as the idea came on, as it dawned on me. And it went on into something, resolved itself into something, to talk about.

And as I was saying to Mr. Dickey as we came, about our lives: What is the thing that you've lived on all the years? Ambition? Yes, ambition of a kind. To get anywhere? No, the ambition was to understand and to have things in poetry and in prose, phrases and certain things, to say back to the world — to say to the bomb, to say to the sphinx; anything from the sphinx to the bomb. Sass it; find something to say.

Understanding; not to have anything come up, in a card game or anything else, that you didn't see what this comes to. [. . .]

Now, just to finish this off a little, that's where you come round to rapid reading. The only rapid reading is skipping what you don't need to read. I can tell by the spine of some books that I can get along without it, and so can everybody else. And a few pages or a page here and there tell me.

The conscientious thoroughness that makes you think you've got to read everything to do it justice, and read every word of it, that's stupid reading, not slow reading. [. . .]

Well, I'll leave that. But the poetry is the basis of it all. That's what we mean. But prose and verse, though — (I'm not saying just rhyme and metre; but prose and verse.) — the essence of it is insight and meaning and purification; clarification, getting rid of the dross, getting down to what this really comes to, taking the bunk out of everything.

Let me say one more thing about poetry, though this doesn't fit into the scheme so much. This occurred to me the other day. I was talking about George Washington, in a foreign country, and I was thinking that the thing about his life was that it contained its own determination, its own terminal. He knew where to stop.

Now, the beauty of everything that we call a "poem" — (In prose or verse, again; I want to be sure about that: prose or verse — or free verse, if they want it that way.) — the thing about a poem is that from the very first sentence in it there's a logic beginning that's going to close it at a certain place. It's got its own closure.

And all the great men that I've thought about in the world, most of them were not like that. They went until somebody else stopped 'em — the way some men go. (You know, some of them go with the ladies that way. They go till they're slapped down.)

The beautiful thing that you call "form" — (It's a beautiful word in athletics, too.) — but as we use it in the arts, the thing is that it has in it the logic of its own termination, conclusion; knows its own stoppage.

And that's what every little poem has. That's what we call "completion." And that doesn't mean the whole universe, but it has its own little completion. [. . .]

When I was here, back there, the first poems I wrote didn't seem to want to close themselves that way. They seemed to end that way, and that was the trouble.

And I always ascribe my experience on a newspaper for a short time — (Very short; enough so that I can boast of being a newspaperman to newspapermen when I meet 'em, and I have to meet 'em pretty often now. You have to have something to say. I ought to bring that in.) — I learned to kind of end things.

I thought texture was everything, just a kind of poetic texture. Whether I made a poem out of it or not didn't bother me. And yet I felt a little troubled. But I had to finish everything on the newspaper, had to run and get it and conclude it.

And I had a little column for a short time — what would be called a "column" now. I wrote paragraphs. They relegated me to that. I wasn't a very good reporter on murders and things like that. And they had me doing a little column on the editorial page, before they called 'em "columns" at all.

And I wrote some little things, paragraphs, that were the beginning of the book of mine I call *North of Boston*, then — little narrative bits out of life that I got. And I learned to finish 'em off. They're in prose, not in verse. This is the way the education came.

No surprise to me,
no surprise to anybody else

The *Eugene Register-Guard* began its coverage of a press conference that preceded Mr. Frost's April 4, 1956, University of Oregon talk, which is excerpted here, by reporting, "Poet Robert Frost, four times a Pulitzer Prize-winner, Tuesday confessed he's never listed his occupation as that of a poet on his income tax returns." The newspaper quoted him as explaining: "I've dodged around it and put down 'farmer' or 'teacher' or 'retired.' I look on 'poet' as a praise word which you don't say about yourself."

I'M ONE of these people that have wished it, when I was teaching, that I only had about ten lectures to give a year. I'd like the privilege in college of giving ten lectures a year — twelve, fifteen at most; something like that.

I'd like never to have to go to a class unless I had something special to report, about what had either happened to me or occurred to me — something special happened or occurred to me; some adventure of the mind or of society, of company.

I can remember thinking I'd say to a class: "What's happened to you since I saw you last? Anything happen to *you*? I'm going to tell you what's happened to *me* — and what's occurred to me, maybe, rather than what's happened to me; that I value more than what's happened to me, what's occurred to me."

And I've tried to teach that way. I've said that that would be "progressive" education in its best sense of the word, if I never told anybody, never told a class, anything that hadn't been something of a surprise to *me*. No surprise to me, no surprise to anybody else. They say, "No tears in the writer, no tears in the reader." And no excitement and no pleasure in the writer, no pleasure in the reader.

That's a curious thing in our day, speaking of the different kinds of people who set up to be as important as I am. Some of them make an agony out of writing and profess their agony. And they expect you to enjoy their agony.

That's a curious contradiction, isn't it? That sounds like Puritanism at the worst. And I take the pleasure in being with you, took the pleasure in making the poems, and take the pleasure in what I've thought of.

Now, just take it as I came in the train. I woke up in the night—this particular thing I'm going to talk about—and I remembered in the night that I'd been bothered a great deal by people's talk about "togetherness"—that horrible word "togetherness." It had crossed me the wrong way.

And I don't go out to fight battles about those things. But it occurred to me that Shelley, when I read him fifty or sixty years ago—(I haven't been looking at him lately, especially. I know some of him by heart. I don't need to look.)—but it occurred to me that he had a poem called "Alastor." And the additional title I'd clean forgot I remembered. I didn't know I knew it. But it occurred to me in the night. Do you know what it is? "Alastor; The Spirit of Solitude." Not togetherness!

This was a poet he was writing about. I remember how it begins:

> There was a Poet whose untimely tomb
> No human hands with pious reverence reared,
> But the charmed eddies of the autumnal wind
> Reared o'er his mouldering bones a pyramid
> Of the waste leaves. . . .

He waste-wandered through the world alone, you know, and died that way. And there he kept solitude all the way. But he

61

was a *poet*. I thought of that in my defense. (This isn't solitude tonight, I admit.) But things occur to me that way.

And I can remember — in my book here, one of the earliest poems I wrote — I can remember just where I was in the street of Lawrence, Massachusetts, when it occurred to me, from having heard about Schopenhauer — (Heard about him; I wasn't reading him at that age. High school I was.) — from having heard about Schopenhauer, that the world — our world, my world, your world, everybody's world — was a product of our will. You see: *The World as Will*. . . . That turned around in my mind.

I remember just where I was in the street. I had one of these things occur to me: that probably I had volunteered to exist — that my own existence was an act of my own will. I volunteered for the particularly bad life I was going to have. It was all read out to me before I was born, and to a number of others. And all of us had a chance to bid on it, and I bid it and went into it. And then I was warned that I wouldn't have the comfort of remembering that I had volunteered. I'd have to live it out, in spite of the fact that I'd forgotten — live it out mystified about what it all had come from and what might have done it, though I had chosen it myself.

So, I made quite a long poem out of that, called "Trial by Existence." I remember just as I walked along the street where that came to me. And that's always been the kind of prompting for the poems and for my talks and for my classes and things.

Many a class I've come to with nothing. And then I just treated it as nothing. I would have earned my pay just as well if I'd only gone twelve times that year to class — where I had something of that kind, that had taken me in a large way by surprise and I couldn't help wanting to make something of it.

I remember hours of it, when I was in a little country academy, high school. I remember days — (Lots of it is all loss to me.) — but I can remember special days when something like that made my hour almost like singing.

People often wonder where the poems come from, and I don't know where they come from, altogether. But that's one of the places they come from. Something that's given, that's come on to me in a sweeping, large way of great surprise.

For instance, to give you another example — (I use this occasionally this way.) — a little while ago it occurred to me — in the night, that way; walking, that time — it occurred to me that no woman had ever made a name, in the world's history in any country, in philosophy. That sounds very anti-feminist, doesn't it? 'Tisn't.

Plato, as I remember, said that *philosophy* belonged up in Athens — among all that crowd, you know, of democrats and things — and *wisdom* belonged down in Sparta. He says so in the *Protagoras*. (This all went through my head.) Wisdom, in other words, in his mind, is not philosophy.

Now, women have wisdom. And they have too much wisdom to be philosophers. That's all that means. (I can get something out of that someday. That wouldn't make a poem necessarily, but it'd make a play. You can get that arranged in three scenes some way and have it out.)

Plato says an amusing thing — (He doesn't mean to be funny ever. I don't remember that he ever looked as if he knew he was funny.) — but he says an amusing thing there. He says that down in Sparta, when they had a visitation of wisdom, when they began to make wisecracks to each other, they put all strangers out of town, so they couldn't profit by them — sayings like, "We all must eat our peck of dirt." You see, that's wisdom. That's wisdom; that isn't philosophy. And "A word to the wise is sufficient." Things like that.

And, oh, let's see: "A cat can look at a king." You see, some woman probably said that. Somebody had been out visiting and seeing everybody, and came home talking about the important people she'd met or he'd met — she'd met, we'll say — and some old lady says, "Well, a cat can look at a king." That was probably said there in Sparta.

And another one, that I've used, probably comes down from Sparta: "Good fences make good neighbors."[22] That's an old, old thing. I didn't get it up. I wish I had.

That's what I'd call "wisdom," not "philosophy." Philosophy is Thales and Anaximander and all that sort of stuff, you know — and Spinoza and other of spinulose stuff. It has its important place — (Let me be careful; probably a philosopher or two in the audience.) — it has its important place as taking, cleansing, purifying religion.

All philosophy has to do with the great God question. And it tries to cleanse. Its object is to cleanse religion of its mere superstition, its grosser superstition. And it's not been quite in vain.

But, you see, the religion is very feminine. In philosophy, the only woman we know of in philosophy hated it. Her name was Xanthippi. She hated it; poured slops out the window on the philosophers when they were talking. That's a fact. It's a fact; that's history.

And then you come to science, and that is more feminine than you'd realize. All science is domestic science — has to do with man's domestication on this planet and our hold on the planet. And as for the laboratories, they're nothing but glorified kitchens.

And then you come to the side where the wisdom is, the sayings of insight, the penetration into life, and that generally comes under the name of "gossip" — rises from our general talk about each other, *guessing* at each other. We guess at each other.

We say, "What's going on there, I wonder?" We guess what's going on there. "Those two have got their heads pretty close together. What's going on there?"

Well, gossip, rising to journalism; then, to chronicle; then, to history; then, to all drama and literature; and finishing off in poetry. But that's all down at that end, very feminine — has to do with men and women altogether.

The religious end, very feminine, too, you know. Well, all you have to do is to think of Eve and Mary — (You see, there are two women.) — and Venus. Eve, Mary, and Venus; makes religion very feminine. This is a feminist talk, you see — just occurred to me!

It's just to show you how these things are made. The talk that I'm making about that now, free and easy and sweeping, someday'll be a long poem, maybe. [. . .]

My wish has been strangely near fulfilled. You see, I'm still a professor, here tonight, teaching. (This is a large class.) I've been growing more and more aware that my dream has been realized, that I only have ten or fifteen or twenty classes a year.

I'll say this, not every one is entirely fresh and new. I can use an idea as it develops — as it develops — and while it's developing I can use it three times. So, three into twenty-one goes seven lectures a year. I suppose it's twenty-one; something like that.

Now, the poems have all got to do with things. There's always a kernel sentence in one of them that is one of these insights that I say belong to the gossip end of life, the wisdom. And I wouldn't value them unless they had that little touch.

Let's take one that was quoted from. The line was, "Earth's the right place for love." That's from one of my poems. I'll say the poem that's in. "Earth's the right place for love: / I don't know where it's likely to go better," I say in the poem. I didn't know when I started the poem I was going to say that. But I came on that flash of the meaning to me, out of much living.

One little sentence like that is out of much living. And that's so hard for some people to understand. It looks so simple, so little. But the triumph of it is that it just comes to a few words out of many days and many, many, many pleasures and pains. [. . .]

[Mr. Frost said his poem "Birches."]

You notice two lines in it that were what probably the Lord was making me write it for — the muse was making me write it for — to get in the line, "It's when I'm weary of considerations." I didn't know I was going to get it in, but something saw that I got that in. And the other was, "Earth's the right place for love: / I don't know where it's likely to go better."

And that's what it's all about, that and the story — the gossip; the gossip; the story. It's gossipy; nature gossip.

—at the University of Minnesota,
October 18, 1961:

I'M ALMOST as interested in education as I am in poetry. [. . .] I've had so much to do with education that I say I'm like some monkeys that Darwin tells about.

He showed them a bagful of snakes. And they looked at 'em and shrieked and threw up their arms and fled. But they couldn't stay away. They kept coming back and looking into the bag at the snakes and throwing up their arms and shrieking and running away again.

That's the way I've done for education, about the last fifty, sixty years — sixty, sixty-five years. And here I am again.

66

Pieces of knitting to go on with

Mr. Frost was the commencement speaker at Colby College on June 11, 1956, and on that occasion was also a recipient of the institution's honorary Doctor of Laws degree.

FIRST I WANT to say to you that up to your graduation, as between entertainment and improvement, the emphasis has been on improvement. If you go on into the graduate schools and so on, it'll be just the same. The emphasis will be on improvement, rather than on entertainment.

But out in the world, as you go, the emphasis will be on entertainment. What entertains you will improve you enough. Adult education that we talk so much about is, as I look at it, more entertainment than anything else.

And, now, when we talk about what's expected of you from now on — assuming that this is the end of schoolwork; assuming that for all of you — what's expected of you is to make some *play* with what you've got jumbled together in your education, out of this department and that department and this course and that course — to kick it round, to be sweeping with it, to be unscrupulous with it — to say it and bid your will about you.

Suppose you're Mr. Nehru in jail, where he wrote his great history of the world. Without any card cases at all or any books to consult, he wrote a history of the world. You may have read it.

And Mr. Toynbee, I don't know just what he did, whether he commanded a card case and all. But, anyway, he took a whole lot of everything that he knew and threw it together and delivered it very sweepingly, so as to leave out anything that wasn't to his purpose. That's what I mean by being "unscrupulous."

Not "corrupt." You see, that's a different word. Not corrupt; but unscrupulous. By unscrupulous I mean not sticking at trifles, in your talk and in your thought. [. . .]

What I mean is that you've picked up a number of interests to go on making play with. Let's put it this way. You have not reached decisions about a good many things. I suppose you have about some. I have about some at my age, a few. And I'm not confused. I have just a certain number of things that I'm picking up every little while as unfinished business.

A woman's name for that is "knitting." A woman carries with her, always has with her — (She ought to have.) — eight or ten pieces of knitting to go on with. And that's what I mean. It's as if you'd picked up here, acquired, eight or ten things to go on with, that you'll pick up at intervals.

For instance, the origin of the species. It's an endless subject. It's been freshened lately by the discovery of one man's jaw — (About eighty years ago, I believe, or so; but the jaw's just got into public.) — a very interesting little jaw. And it's possible to reason from it that we didn't come from the apes or the monkeys at all. We came from the lemurs, those creatures with big innocent eyes. That might be us.

But that goes on. That I don't consider conclusive. That's my knitting, my unfinished business. I'll always be thinking about it. Another one that I'll always be picking up now and then, to go on with a little way, is the immortality of the soul.

Now, that doesn't mean changing my opinion. That means picking up or having or hearing, listening to, an idea on the subject. Sometimes it's a humorous one. Sometimes it's a deeper one.

A friend said to me, rather sadly, about that the other day, he said: "As I get older, I seem to be playing in more luck in this world. And you know what I think? It's because I have a larger party in heaven; so many of my friends have gone there." That's what I mean by having an idea on the subject.

Another idea, less touching than that: "What's grandma reading the Bible so much for lately?" somebody said. "She's cramming for her finals."

Things you think of for yourself that add to it, that come in on that theme. That theme is, you see, picked up again.

Now, the one I wanted to say the most about was a "dream." I don't know how much you've come across it in your courses. But I'm always coming across it — in public, in editorials and places — that there was a "dream." And there's always this tone about it as if it hadn't been fulfilled or quite fulfilled.

There was a "dream." A poem puts it this way:

> For each age is a dream that is dying,
>   Or one that is coming to birth.[23]

Now, the question right away is: What is an age? How long is an age? Is our dream, our American dream — that I think Dreiser thought was "an American tragedy" — is that dream over? And are we on a new dream?

Or is the Constitution something that isn't performing — a sort of a vanishing act, fading as we watch it, and turning into something else? When they call it a "living document," that means they can have it any way they want it for this generation. That's the danger. [. . .]

I know many of my friends who consider themselves right to be disappointed in the dream, just as Henry Adams was. That fella! He did more toward disillusionment about the dream than Dreiser did, because he did it more exquisitely, more beautifully, in writing.

But he considered himself justified in his disappointment. He gave everything a chance to educate him. He gave Harvard a chance. He gave America a chance. He gave the world a chance. He gave God a chance. And you had to admit that he was something worth educating. But they couldn't educate him. America failed him.

Well now, again, as you come across it. People say to me: "I don't think the dream has come true. It has merely 'materialized.'" You see, like a ghost or something.

That's a dangerous word. In a visit abroad last year — southward a way; South America — at a convention I heard nothing but that charge — that anxiety for us, for the world — that the American dream had merely materialized, and materialized grossly.

Well, I'm not here to decide that for you. I simply present it as a piece of knitting to go on with.

Let me say what I'd do about it if I were you. Right now, while the Supreme Court is making decisions between confederacy and union, I'd go back and read some of the "Federal Papers." I'd go back and see whose dream it was. Plenty of time, you've got it all before you. There's a whole lot of it in it.

Was it George Washington's dream? Was it Thomas Jefferson's dream? Was it Tom Paine's dream? Was it Gouverneur Morris's dream? Those people were all thinking about it, and a good deal at loggerheads about it.

And then for me — to tell you how far I've got on my knitting — (I haven't finished it; it's still unfinished business with it.) — for me the man that comes the nearest what I think was the dream, that may be ours still, was Madison. In the "Federal Papers," go to Madison and see what he thought it was going to be.

What was it going to be? Go along and think about that — using the "think" in the slang: "You've got another think coming." You see? I've got another think coming. But that's what I mean. You have these things to go on with.

I would think that Tom Paine was very little in it. I was with a friend just two nights ago who is a Tom Paine-ite. He said, "It's all Tom Paine." But, no; not for me.

I've read a good deal of Tom Paine, and I know a good deal of what he thought. He thought that there was something started about the brotherhood of man that was going to set the whole world on fire, sweep the world.

So, he rushed right off to France about it. And we see what came of it. They had a revolution there. And they've had four republics — and not to mention three or four monarchies — since then. Their dream was a very confused dream, if they had a dream.

Another thing that I pick up — (I don't want to be too decisive about it.) — about freedom and equality. It occurred to me not so terribly long ago — rather recently — that the more equality I have, the less freedom I have. Those two things balance each other.

If one party leans a little more toward the freedom — freedom of enterprise, freedom to assert yourself, freedom to achieve, freedom to win — the other comes in with the tone of mercy and says: "Let's not let anybody get too far ahead. Let's have a Sherman Act or something, to keep people from getting too rich." That's toward the equality, the fraternity of it.

I didn't know that for years, didn't know that the more freedom I had, the less equality I could expect — somebody'd beat me and get ahead of me if we have freedom. (I'm willing to let him get ahead of me, if he can.)

Now, just for the fun of it — winding this up — the theme is, you see, the knitting, the unfinished business — the many pieces of knitting; the half a dozen or dozen. I don't know how many. I'm not going to spend the time on that. I spent the time on two or three, just to indicate what you'll pick up and go on with.

You won't lie awake nights about it. And if you lie awake

nights from too much coffee, you might pick one of these up. But you won't be lying awake on purpose for that.

And probably the best you do with that unfinished business is when you aren't putting your mind too intensely on them. You just pick 'em up and have another think about them. And sometimes you think of something amusing.

For instance, I remember thinking once that all men are created *equally funny*. That was a step forward for me. That, anyway, comes in: equally absurd.

—*at Hill School, November 5, 1961:*

It used to be a consideration with me, when I was teaching in an academy, to find the handle end of poetry —handle end. Now I think that I was wrong in hunting for it: What would be the handle end of poetry, the thing to get hold of?

But I don't think it was necessary to look for that particularly. I think you've got the handle end with you. It must be very few of you haven't found poetry and rhyming rather catchy. You know what a catchy couplet is and a catchy rhyme, a lucky rhyme. [. . .]

Looking back at a freshman class now and then in college, I wonder how many of them entered into poetry a little in this way, before ever they started to study it. I've tried to find that out sometimes: if they entered into it at home. [. . .]

For me as a teacher it always was: What's the best handle I can offer them for the whole thing in poetry? I should think the best handle was rhymes, couplets, and lucky words and lucky sentences.

Everything in the world comes in pairs

In beginning this talk to the students at Phillips Exeter Academy on October 11, 1956, Mr. Frost made mention of H. Darcy Curwin, a member of the academy's English Department.

THE SUREST THING you know is that everything in the world comes in pairs that you're living between in great uncertainty. You have two certainties that are always there. They are the surest thing you know. I'm very sure that your life between them is a daily uncertainty that the psychologists can't do anything about.

Now, I was led to think of that by a line in my own verse that Mr. Curwin had me write today. "When I was young my teachers were the old," the poem begins. "I gave up fire for form till I was cold."[24]

Now, fire and form, inspiration and know-how. You see, you're between inspiration and know-how. You're between fire and form. And you have a feeling as you come along in school, the further you get, they've taken all the feeling out of you and given you in exchange for it a certain amount of know-how.

And you wouldn't believe it, maybe — (I'm speaking to the right age here.) — you might not believe it, but you'll get worried about that sometime in your life. I get worried about it now. I think I know too much for my spirit.

It's like a volcano that runs fire, but it crusts on itself and checks itself with its own crust and has to break crust again to flow — flows and crusts and flows and crusts. And everything you're doing in writing and thinking, all your learning and every-thing, has that about it.

It's too easy for my enemies to say, at my age that I know how too well, that I'm doing it on my know-how — the way you might play tennis on your inspiration when you're young and when you can get about everywhere, on all parts of the court at once. And then the day comes when you just have to stand in one place and do it on your old foxiness, your know-how.

You can see that happening in the sports; see a man outlast himself a little while on his know-how — outlast himself. And the poets have that same thing, as I have said.

Now, that's just one thing. Let's take another one that you're always going to spend your life worrying about — another uncer-tainty — about selfishness and unselfishness.

In school it comes this way. Let me tell you about a poem I read for years without noticing a certain word in it:

> My heart leaps up when I behold
> A rainbow in the sky . . .

And he goes on to say at the end of it — (I'm only here to recite my own poems!) — he goes on to say at the end of it:

> I could wish my days to be
> Joined . . .

"Bound each to each" is it or "Joined . . ."?—

> Joined each to each by natural piety.[25]

Now, "natural piety" to me for years and years meant only a piety that's natural to have, piety to God or anything. But it doesn't mean that. It means piety toward nature. And it never occurred to me for years and years and years.

And I'm so selfish in my nature, in my ego, that I'm glad I

waited all those years to find it out for myself and never had it pointed out to me by a teacher. That's the selfishness of it, you see. And I'd ten times rather go without a lot of knowledge than have it pointed out to me.

And that's so in my own poems. Somebody says to me, "I see what you mean, but just what are you driving at?" (That's, "What's ulterior there?") And I don't want to have to tell that. And I'd think everybody'd be selfish enough to want to see that for himself.

And I look at a lot of our teaching as a kind of trespass on a lofty selfishness that young people ought to have.

Don't tell me. Somebody gives me a conundrum, and I can see he's so anxious to tell me, that I don't have a chance to think it out for myself. It makes me nervous, and I give in quickly, of course, to please his selfishness. He means to tell me.

I want to be left alone. I want to make my own observations and have my own experience. This is speaking of books, and so out in life, too.

But I know that I should be unselfish enough to let people tell me some things — teachers and professors and friends and relatives; and enemies, as well as friends.

You could go on multiplying. I'll tell you another, one of the vastest uncertainties of our time. The two opposites that you're sure of, one is called "civilization" and the other is — its opposite — is "utopia."

Now, you think that over, and you'll see that every time you vote you're voting between utopia and civilization. Civilization means *all* the freedoms, even the dangerous freedoms, the risky freedoms. And the utopia means security.

You want some security, you know. And you want some civilization; you want some risk. Everybody is in the same difficulty. Every day is an uncertainty — especially election day. [. . .]

I have a feeling that many people that get educated, they get into a state of pressing everything too hard for meaning. They get discouraged about it all. They get afraid that there's something there that they aren't educated enough to see. Give 'em one more year in college, and they must know how to read it — or one more teacher. There's a cowardice about that, isn't there?

I see a boy looking at a poem of mine, and I see he's encountered it before. He's looking at it hard, and he's still worried about it. How much he would like help from me, instead of being brave about it and saying never mind what I do mean. [. . .]

And there's another one that you're lost between: carefulness — rightness, exactness — and not sticking at trifles. Another word for not sticking at trifles is "unscrupulousness." Will you act a little unscrupulous? And how unscrupulous will you be?

Unscrupulous is not sticking at trifles. That's all it means. Scruples, little things. (You don't want to have what they call "a soul for buttons." You don't want to be bothered by buttons — not in a day of zippers, anyway!)

But there you are, between those two. Between generosity, that is a kind of a largeness about things, and meanness, that is suspicious and careful and all that. You're there, and you want to be a little mean, I suppose.

How mean you want to be? And how generous you want to be? You don't want to be so generous that you throw yourself away. And the government doesn't want to be so generous that it throws itself away. (I'll be talking politics before I know it. Best to keep out of that.)

Well, I'll leave that now and say some poems to you. Just that one thing that I'm telling you about: The certainties are double; always a pair of certainties that you're uncertain between, every day, every minute — friendship, trust; faith, unfaith.

It says, "Lord, I believe" — (And what's the next, in the same

76

breath?)—"help thou mine unbelief."[11] Belief/unbelief; and you're there between those two or you're not alive.

What your education is toward is, I'd say, two things. One is action, achievement. And that can begin any time after you're fourteen or fifteen or sixteen or seventeen—(Somewhere along there it begins.)—in the arts and in science and mathematics and all these things.

The kind of selfishness I talk of begins where you want to do it for yourself and achieve something for yourself. That begins much younger than you'd think. Very young you ought to begin to be a little resentful of people who want to impose too much on you.

You don't want to contradict anybody, but you want to be in this state of wanting to do it as much as possible for yourself, with a little touch of generosity toward others. You know, an unselfishness; and let 'em tell you a little. Don't let 'em tell you too much.

I might say that it's the same for poetry, the same for science. The advertisements in the *Scientific America* are all for young men and women that want to be original in science. They're advertising for 'em. I thought science had stolen the show—because it has all these atoms—I thought it had stolen the show, and it hasn't. They're advertising, themselves, that they aren't getting boys enough.

I said: "Where are they going? They've left poetry, I'm pretty sure. Where have they all gone? Haven't they gone to science?" "No," they say, "they've gone to sociology." So I hear.

But this thing in science, just the same, this selfishness. Not too selfish; but it's selfishness. It's do it yourself and get up something and be among the originators of things. Don't let the Germans all do it and the British all do it. (Who gave us jet propulsion? Who gave us penicillin? Who gave us a lot?)

We won't prolong this. But, you know, I'm a little unselfish. I want the other nations to do some of it, but I wish we were doing more of it. And I want everybody that goes to M.I.T. to keep away from the culture courses and go far in science — (Tell 'em I said so!) — and way, way up, you know, where the originality is, what they call "pure science."

In the advertisements they don't like to say "pure." That doesn't sound nice in an advertisement. But they say "basic science." Basic science, that means the same thing — the high; not gadgeteering and engineering, but science, basic science.

It has the same quality that poetry has about it, asks the same thing of you. Two things that make it are the selfishness that wants to be the ones that think it, and the other is a tendency to make metaphor all the time, to seek connections and relations all the time. And that belongs to poetry just the same as it does to science.

—at Johns Hopkins University,
November 9, 1958:

LATELY I've heard a lot of talk about the Supreme Court. And that set me to thinking, drawing a line between the umpire or the referee — (This broadens out a little into all the sports: the referee/umpire.) — and the handicapper.

No referee, no umpire has a right to be a handicapper. He has no right to say that the underdog needs a little help. So, now you're in the question of the Supreme Court that will bear watching — (I don't mean the question will bear watching, I mean the Supreme Court will bear watching.) — to see whether they sharply make that division between being referee, with no interest especially in upperdog or underdog. That's for the handicapper; and that's for Congress and the President.

My kind of fooling

In an appearance at Harvard University on December 3, 1956, held under the auspices of its Morris Gray Poetry Fund, Mr. Frost made near the beginning of his remarks a reference to the celebrated portrait painter Charles Hopkinson (1869–1962), who lived in the North Shore area of Massachusetts and maintained a studio at Boston.

I THOUGHT I would begin today in a way I heard another poet friend of mine begin once. He said, "This is the first time I have declared myself in public on the subject of——" Well, I've changed the subject; never mind what his subject was. But this is the first time I have declared myself in public on the subject of whom I'm writing these poems for.

This was brought up in my mind by Mr. Hopkinson, the artist. He asked me how near I felt to the audience I'm writing to. And he meant me to ask him how near he felt to the man whose portrait he was painting. That's pretty close up, isn't it? Mine is certainly more remote than that. [. . .]

But it's a question that I'm often asked: who I'm writing the poems for.

Some singer said the other day — in answer to the question which she liked of her own songs best — she said, "The one you like." Nice answer.

Which one of my poems do I like best? The one I heard last praised. And that's no jest, though you laugh. It's true that I am very happy about a poem for a few hours after I've heard it praised, quite a little while — maybe all night; sleep well on it.

But when you ask me further, I think I can say. I can give

you some idea. I wrote it for all the nice people I've been thrown with. And I've been thrown with some pretty nice ones, intelligent and free and happy — know how to take my kind of play in conversation.

Probably my education was in conversation, all the way along, without my knowing it. I said in verse somewhere:

> It takes a lot of in- and outdoor schooling
> To be admitted to my kind of fooling.[26]

I certainly write for what you might call "a cloud of witnesses," a cloud of people that I've been thrown with — not definitely for any person or any kind of person. I certainly don't write for the kind of people that enjoy looking up my references. Not particularly for them; I don't mind them.

But suppose, as in one poem I'm going to read you today, I mention "Igdrasil." I'd rather you didn't have to look it up. I'd rather; that's just preference.

I do this on a percentage basis, as I often say. Some get one thing and some another. But the things you get on the spot are the things that I want you to get, that I enjoy your getting most. The pleasure I have is from the things you respond to at once.

Now, do I write the poems to read them aloud? I write them to my ear, certainly, my own ear. I write them to the ear — (I would hate to admit I didn't.) — that before anything else, probably. So, it ought to be that I write them to be read aloud.

But I recognize a considerable difference. Some of them I don't dare to read aloud. They're too intimate maybe or too something, you know. I have a feeling that they'd be helped by your seeing them, as well as hearing them.

In fact, I went so far once as to get my publishers to make me a little pamphlet of half a dozen of them, that I could distribute to an audience at the door — give out at the door — so that people would have the help of the eye in hearing me read them. And the trouble with that was everybody wanted my autograph on them afterward. That had to be stopped; didn't go any further, one audience.

But the great thing is my metaphor. That's my kind of fooling. That's what I mean by "my kind of fooling" — my kind of metaphor, my kind of double meaning, double entendre, intimation, innuendo, insinuation, simile; anything you want to call it. ("Symbol" is the dread word you were waiting for!) And I suppose each has his own kind.

I understand that over at Technology now they've introduced a whole lot of cultural courses. Fifty percent now, you can take going through there, fifty percent cultural. And that's so's to get 'em ready for my kind of fooling. That must be it. And that means my kind of play with the metaphor.

I encountered one of them, head on, the other day, one of the M.I.T. scientists; interesting man. We tried to come to an understanding about the metaphor. And we didn't succeed, not very well. It would take more time. He felt a little standoffish with me, suspicious of me.

I claimed that all science — everything, all advances in everything — rested on this little expression you can make a singsong out of: "How she differs from what she's like." You see, "How she differs from what she's like."

The order, you know, would be "what she's like," first. And then where the metaphor breaks down is where the progress is. That's the way science is advanced, I'm sure. But that was news to him. Probably we'd mean the same thing after an hour or two of it; didn't have long enough.

His great difficulty about poetry was — and regular verse — was that it purposely "handicapped" itself. I didn't say to him, but right away he's used a metaphor, hasn't he: handicap? And a bad one and a vulgar one!

You see, that's what that is: that I assume the responsibilities of form, as in any game or as anywhere you look.

For instance, is it a handicap in a race to say that it shall be a mile long? No, that's not a handicap, is it? That would be a dreadful use of it. There's the mile, two miles, the hundred yards, and so on.

Those are forms — no handicap to be thought of, unless there's somebody butts in to place one person two or three feet ahead of somebody else, as in a Sunday-school picnic. In the horse races they do. It hurts all that. That's handicapping.

But he brought that into the whole thing. He said, "Why *do* you rhyme, then, and why *do* you use metre?" I said, "From the craving I have for form — for something that rounds it out, that shapes, you know."

But he still said he thought that I was handicapping myself. I said, "Well, I'm handicapping myself, if you want to put it that way, in using the English language." You see, all those words, why should I use them? [. . .]

I said: "You don't come into the world to find out whether it's a good world or not. You come into it to find out whether you're any good *at it* — to try yourself; not to try the world, but to try yourself — just as you come onto a tennis court not to find out whether it's a good court, but to find out whether you can play tennis."

He couldn't say much to that. He couldn't say "handicap" to that. That broke down his metaphor.

Well, that's the whole story.

I'd like to say one thing more that I care about. I wish in all my poems that people listen to, that they hear something of the voice — more than the words, more than the vowels and the consonants — something that changes in every sentence and something that I like to think no notation could indicate; there's no help for it but the context of the story or the verse.

Suppose I just show you — away from a poem — a little case of it. I asked a friend of mine if another friend of mine was really crazy. And he said, "Well, you know."

You see, now that's enough. I knew a lot from that tone when he said, "Well, you know." You see? Now, how much more do I need to add to that? That tone does it.

Somebody said, "Well, if it were me, I would have run this campaign in another way." He thought a minute, and he said, "I would have *winked* at what the French and British and Jews were doing." See, all the tone of that, where he sounded very wicked. (I would have winked, too. Talking politics now!)

Let's see if I think of another one. Milton says somewhere, makes one of the brothers say ——

Oh, say, just speaking of Milton, do you suppose Milton wrote all that stuff so you'd have to look up a lot of things in it? You know, I don't assume that he did. But I don't feel sure of him. I'm sure Shakespeare didn't write anything for you to look anything up about. And I'm sure Chaucer didn't.

I can't think of writing purposely to have anybody look anything up. I'm not sure of Milton. You see the way I say that, too, you know — humbly. I don't suppose I know. I'm among a lot of scholars here.

I was going to give you an example from Milton. One of the brothers says to another two nice questions, such natural questions that they break in on you in the middle of a great deal of sort of almost pompous English. But it says in one place, "Shall I go on?" — one brother says to the other — "Shall I go on? / Or have I said enough?"[27]

What two pretty questions those are, for their tone of voice. They're right in the blank verse, too. "Shall I go on?" I say to you — (I said that once in class years ago, and I said it so naturally that one of the boys said, "Go on.") — "Shall I go on? / Or have I said enough?"

83

Take another place in Milton — (I like to take Milton, because it is on that high plane. You won't think it's colloquial ever.) — he says:

> Begin then, Sisters of the sacred well,
> That from beneath the seat of Jove doth spring,
> Begin, and somewhat loudly sweep the string.

And then he says:

> Hence with denial vain, and coy excuse. . . .

That sentence always delighted me:

> Hence with denial vain, and coy excuse. . . .[28]

Don't say you've got a cold. Or don't say you can't sing. Or don't say you can't please us. It's in Shakespeare you get that, you know. He says, "I know I can't please you." And the other fellow says, with a beautiful tone of voice, "We don't ask you to please us." He says, "We just ask you to sing."[29]

It's all that play of those tones that I like to think people are hearing when I read to them or when they read me themselves. It's a great temptation to go colloquial, just on that account. I remember an old colloquial poem about an old woman who was asked if she was ready to die. And she says, "As ready as I'll ever be, I reckon." — "As ready as I'll ever be, I reckon."[30] Just hear it.

Now I'm going to read to you. But one of the things they say to me is, "You don't dare to read 'em new things." (Did I write 'em to read 'em right off, or did I write for them to get around in the anthologies first, so they'll get ready for me to read 'em aloud?) So, I'm going to take my courage in hand today. This is the first time I've done that on a challenge. I'm going to dare to read you something a little too new to be read.

All right? Not the first thing, I'll start with something else.

I don't want to go back to the old ones. I want to take some of the later ones.

Oh, I tell you one. I will go back to one early one, for this reason. It has in it the real line of why I write the poems. Do I write 'em for me? Do I write 'em for you? Or do I write 'em into the wastebasket?

You know, I never could decide that. This poem will help you, make you see, I think. [. . .]

This is a little farming poem that has in it one line that gives you my position, probably, all the years of my life. I wrote it back in the nineties — fifty years ago, anyway, and maybe more. It's about mowing in the morning.

The mower in the morning mowed when the grass was wet, with his scythe, because it made the cutting easier — just as shaving is easier when 'tisn't dry. And I came after the mower in the dew, as a boy, and I tossed the grass out to dry in the sun, shake the dew out of it and open it up to the sun. And that's the surface of it.

It's called, though, "A Tuft of Flowers." You see, what's that doing in the mowing poem, a tuft of flowers? That's the real secret of it all. [. . .]

> [Mr. Frost said the opening twenty-six lines
> of "The Tuft of Flowers"; then, interjected:]

And this is the place:

> Nor yet to draw one thought of ours to him,
> But from sheer morning gladness at the brim.

That's the source of it all. I'll finish the poem, but that's where I wanted to get you.—

> The mower in the dew had loved them thus,
> By leaving them to flourish, not for us . . .

That's the way the poems are written.—

> Nor yet to draw one thought of ours to him,
> But from sheer morning gladness at the brim. . . .

[Mr. Frost then completed his saying of the poem.]

—at Emerson College, May 7, 1959:

I suppose I ought to say something about poetry and its audibility, its being heard. Someone told me the other day that we've got to get the resonance out of poetry. And I think that'd be the end of poetry.

If they want to get it out, they should write it as algebraic equations. There'd be no resonance in them. (And it's getting down to that, somewhat.)

But when resonance goes, I go. My interest has always been to the ear first.

Of course, much depends on the thought.

One danger is of thinking that by sound and resonance we mean vowels and consonants and all that. We mean the tones of meaning that come from having ideas.

—at Princeton University, December 5, 1956:

One thing I like to be in this world is so sweeping —you see, get along so sweepingly—that I can't fall down.

And I don't want to get bogged down with thoroughness, do I? And I don't want to get kind of lost —(Bewildered, you might say.)—bewildered with diffuseness.

About "the great misgiving"

In beginning his April 10, 1958, lecture to the Great Issues Course at Dartmouth, Mr. Frost spoke of having at last fixed upon the designation for a collection of his poems that had not yet been brought forth in book form. It would, however, be another four years before the long-anticipated volume was finally published — carrying as its title *In the Clearing*.

W HAT I'M GOING to talk about is something I've been working toward. I always have a hard time naming a book, and it's about time I had another book. My publishers expect one of me every seven years, but it's past seven now. I've got to have a book for 'em pretty soon.

But I've been stalling. And they think from just laziness and good-for-nothingness, that I just can't come to a point. But the real fact is I have to feel something that kind of — just for me, privately — pulls the book together.

They're scattered poems that I write, around. People think I wrote a book called *North of Boston* and wrote it as a book. I didn't. It's just scattered poems that I pulled together under the head *North of Boston*. And it looks very well, even to outsiders, as a name. But usually the name means just something to me. It's my reason to finally close the book and get it off my hands.

And I've finally got to it. Take you in on this: I've finally decided to call the book *The Great Misgiving*. You'd have to look far into the book to find what I mean by that. But I'll tell you a little about it, what it means to me.

If I could, I'd have handed you for this affair just a little

87

map, of about the size of this, of the whole world. (What I think they call a "Mercator's Projection." Is that the old name for it?) This would be the whole world, spread out here, exaggerated at both poles. It's spread too wide at both poles, but it's just map enough for us.

And then I'd ask you to make on it a black mark. It wouldn't be much longer than ten inches. And it would begin in the west coast of Asia Minor, and it would stretch, black and rather broad, right across the Aegean, across Greece, across Italy, across Germany. It would be wide enough to take Germany, France, England — and then on to us; just to us.

This thing would be stretching west-northwest, sort of. And there'd be nothing else like it on the map. There couldn't be anything else like it. It's the only place where this belongs, this thing. It's like a cinder path.

I'll tell you where "the great misgiving" comes in. Only two peoples, Eastern and Western, have had this great misgiving. It belongs to us and becomes us, Eastern and Western — east of that place where I begin the black line and west of it to us; beginning, I like to say, around the Land of Moab or somewhere where the alphabet did — starting from scratch on the Moabite Stone. It's a kind of a cinder track — starting from scratch on the Moabite Stone; if you get that.

And there's nothing like it went the other direction. And Africa's got nothing to do with it. If there's anything of this in Africa, it's for the far future; we don't know.

But this misgiving that becomes us was taken in two ways, the Western way and the Eastern way. [. . .] We have taken it our way, and they have taken it their way. And our way is as much as to say, "The greatest merit of all is to risk the spirit in substantiation, in plunging into matter." That's the greatest merit of all.

The second greatest merit would be so worried about the spirit that you'd just clasp your hands and drop on your knees and wait till you're dead, for fear your spirit should be lost in a material world. That's the Eastern way, waiting for Nirvana, hoping not to get born again — hoping not to get born again into this bad world. That's the Eastern way. I presume to call that second best.

It's well that we should have this misgiving, this fear for the spirit. And I've been saying lately to graduate schools when I met them: "Don't ever let me hear you fellows in the graduate school talk about 'materialism.' You're more in danger of losing the spirit of what you're dealing, in your material, than almost anybody else."

It's the curse of the graduate school, that they get lost in their own material. They think their duty is material, of course. But of course the duty of all of us is to enter into the material. I've got to substantiate my claim to being here this morning, substantiate it. I've got to materialize it. (I want a different word for it from "materialism." It's "materiality.")

I enter into the material every poem I write, every talk I make. I enter into the material, at the risk of the spirit. We recognize the spirit in various ways, by a show of vanity maybe (sometimes no more than that), by wit, by ideas — by *meaning*; that's the height of it all.

It's a great wonder to me that the books produced in the graduate school are not thought meaningful enough for anybody to want to buy 'em, in this material world. That's just speaking of them.

But the whole thing is that. And I say in verses in the book, a verse that goes like this:

> Even God's descent
> Into flesh . . .

See, God descended into flesh, according to our Christian religion.—

> . . . God's descent
> Into flesh was meant
> As a demonstration
> That the supreme merit
> Lay in risking spirit
> In substantiation.[31]

He had to substantiate; that is, He had to give meaning to the world.

Now, the two ways that you've got. One is to fear it so much, have the misgiving so strong, that you clasp your hands and just pray to be saved from this gross material world. And the other is — (We have a slang word, don't we? I don't know whether you ever heard it.) — the Western way has been to "duff" in. You see, duff in — (I presume that's the same word as you get in "plum duff" and such as that; "duff into the dough.") — go for it; go for the material, knowing the risk, feeling the risk.

The church has a lot to do with that misgiving, of course. Sometimes the church has stalled it. It's had a stalling effect, it's been so afraid of the material.

But, now, make this picture on the map, this charge, this great charge into the material that began with the alphabet, partly — "the greatest analysis of all analyses," somebody said. Only once in the world.

These are the wonderful things, that these are so individual. Some man must have said — somewhere there on that coast or somewhere near Moab — said to himself, "Look at all these words we say." He didn't know how many they were. But he said: "Look at all these words we say. If you stop to analyze them, they can all be reduced to twenty sounds."

Wasn't that a feat of analysis? Nobody else ever did it. The

90

East never did it. This happened right on that verge there, coming our way.

That was the part of the thing that gave the spirit its chance, a written language. A B C and 1 2 3, those two things had so much to do with it.

But this venture into the material that I call "materiality," not "materialism," was an adventure of the spirit into matter, to see if the spirit couldn't be kept. And it's kept wherever there's meaning kept. And it's lost wherever it goes into just a dump of material.

I was running my eye over a bookcase just before I came, and I saw so many titles — ('Twas books of this time, they seemed to be.) — so many titles that showed this that I could call this "misgiving," this fear of being lost in the material.

I'm going to see somebody in Washington who's brother I remember seeing years ago out in Wyoming, up at Laramie, up seven thousand feet nearer heaven. He said to me — (A fine man; he put his hand to his head.) — "I'm confused, aren't you?" That's what he meant, you know; he was losing the meaning.

And when you talk about "existentialism," it just means that. (The word for it in the church is "acedia.") It's a spirit giving up. An existentialist is a person that wouldn't be bothered to commit suicide. He wouldn't be bothered. And the thing is, it's the failure — just for him and all around him, as he sees it — the failure of the spirit; that there isn't meaning enough to anything for him to go on with it. [. . .]

I'm not here to find fault, am I? And all I'm saying is that the meaning when lost is "acedia" or "existential" or whatever you want to call it — acedia or existential.

Now, picture it this way, again on this map — this cinder path that I've made across it. It's been the great adventure into the material, at the risk of the spirit. And I call it "materiality," unless it fails; and then I call it "materialism."

If I succeed with my material — in writing a poem or in making a speech — if I succeed with my material, I'm dealing with the material, of course, and I'm a material artist. And if I fail, I'm a saddened, sad materialist; that's all.

And so with your being at college, your being anywhere. Your being in Washington; your being President of the United States — when you lie alone at night, the thing that concerns you, the misgiving, is whether you're making this almost unwieldy mass, the United States — with a hundred and sixty million people — whether you're putting something into it, and whether you can go before Congress tomorrow and help put some meaning into it.

And one of the amusing things to me is that the Eastern world has just sort of been lately waked up to our way of doing it. And they've started wondering if ours isn't the better way to take the misgiving. They've taken it one way, and we've taken it another. And they've come West to find out whether our way is better than their way.

Maybe theirs is better. Maybe I better not say. I think ours is better, probably. That's in my heart. But it might be we're wrong. Maybe the best way is to go into a cell somewhere and pray our time out. Or will we *plunge*? Will we go on with the plunging way?

It's somewhere in the poem, the longish poem somewhere in the book, that I take the title from:

> Westerners inherit
> A design of living
> Deeper into matter . . .

You see:

> Deeper into matter —
> Not without some patter
> Of the great misgiving.[31]

92

You see, always worrying about the spirit — as we should. Have we kept it? Are we keeping it? And that's without getting religious about it at all. I brought God into it, but the point is just *meaning*, plain meaning.

There are lulls in it, when you're scared entirely. There are lulls in your life, when you wonder what it's all about — what it's all about. Are you acting as if you had some clue to what it's about — some clue?

It needn't come too clear, but the very confidence you have in being here, the very confidence you have in not committing suicide, means that you think there's some sort of meaning. There's something to go on with — in fear and trembling. [. . .]

I belong to the West. I'm not interested in the detachment and the dispassionateness that saves a man from getting born again. That's the Eastern way, to get off the wheel. You know, according to that, even when you're an angel, you're not safe. You can get born again and be a monkey. You gotta look out. And the way out of it is detachment, this fear of the material that detaches you from everything, takes the passion all out of your life, the passion for science or for everything — for action; the passion for action.

Finish the picture; then I'll change the subject. This cinder path, starting from scratch on the Moabite Stone, makes it a sort of a hundred-yard dash that the Western race has made, right across Greece and all — (Call it a hundred-yard dash.) — to us, ending in a pole vault — always in fear for everything; fear for the track, fear for yourself and everything.

Physical condition has something to do with it, too. You'd think it might not be. If you got sick enough you might write like an existentialist, I suppose, and might prevail that way, sick-spirited.

Remember the church has that wonderful word about it.

It's so old, that "acedia." Look it up. See how deep a meaning it had for monks and priests and for the church.

Only the great people of the world have had the misgiving, East and West. And they've taken it two ways. And whether ours is the right way or theirs is the right way is for someone else to say. I'm not saying. I incline. I'm Western, sort of. But it might be that we could be wrong about it. Maybe we're going to lose the spirit, in this "derring do."[31]

I've lived longer than you have. I met the people that made the "pole vault," the Wright brothers. Look at us now. But that's all into the material. That's all; it's a venture of the spirit into the material.

Do we carry meaning with it? Is the spirit with it? Always scare yourself once in a while for fear it isn't in your work, isn't in your life.

There are prescribed ways in the world for being kind of sure that you're doing something that means something. You can be a doctor or lawyer or Indian chief, you know — some of those things; something that you fall into that has sort of meaning already, been given meaning — and teaching and writing poetry and coaching teams. [. . .]

It's dangerous for me to say any poems after that, isn't it? Because, have I put enough meaning into them? I'm a materialist, and the most physical part of my poems are the parts I like best, where they're really *physical*. There are other words for that, but I like it: "physical."

But it's got to go beyond that. Take a matter like this. We know that the one thing that's a sign of a real person is that he wants to win. Whether he plays cards or whether he goes into games or into a word contest or something, but he likes to win. Then, he has to find out what it means to win.

In some of these subjects you study, what is winning?

Is "A" winning — or "B" winning enough? Is that really victory?

The Romans dragged Christians to the altar of victory. If they wouldn't bow down to that, they fed 'em to the lions. But they wanted 'em to bow to the idea of victory. [. . .] That's vitality, to want to win.

But now beyond that — to give that meaning — beyond that is not to be made a fool of by winning or by losing, either. (You can be made a fool of by both.) And then you get up into the spiritual, where the high meaning is, and you say: "Well, what do I want more than victory? Well, I want to behave myself in victory or defeat, 'cause you can have either."

This is where the spiritual begins. You say: "Why do I want to behave myself? It's expected of me." Just say that much. "It seems to be expected of me that I shan't be made a fool of by either victory or defeat." And now you're up in the spiritual world. And the next thing you know you're at the top of the Golden Stairs.

—at Goucher College, November 29, 1950:

NOBODY EVER told me anything about my poems that made me write anything any different. [. . .]

My best critic is the other poems that have been written. Every little while I clear my eyes all away and take a fresh look at something that others have written in the past. [. . .]

And then sometimes I go directly from something somebody else has written, other things, and look at mine with that same desire to be clear and face it. And that's about all it ever amounts to. That's the only criticism I ever know.

Wondering how convictions are had

Robert Frost's 1958 visit to the University of California at Berkeley involved his speaking and reading on May eighth in the open-air setting of the campus's Greek Theatre.

CALIFORNIA HAS the two great fames, Hollywood and science, the world over. And it's always my longing that it should come up into having its own literary centers out here. San Francisco ought to be one of them.

And now this is my chance to say that some newspaper quite perversely made a heading out of my misgivings about the young poets, the "Beat Generation."

I had hardly seen the poems. And I'd seen enough of them to see that they were "mis'able," as we say in New England. But, but, but — I added that if it was genuine misery, not affected, it was all right with me. (If any of them are here or anywhere around, in the slums or wherever they are, I hope this reaches them, in my friendliness about it.)

I've lived through of course many, many things like this, little movements that you think much might come of, and so seldom anything comes of them.

Now, I'm not going to talk to you very long. But in this open daylight, it seems as if I could hardly tell you what my greatest interest in the young people over the country is. It seems as if, looking at all this lightness here and all of you spread around, there couldn't be many who suffered what I suffered from when I was of the college age.

I suffered from wondering how convictions are had — how you have 'em. I saw older people with them. And I saw older people worried because I seemed to have none. And I worried about it a little myself.

It's that kind of youth that seems to be my greatest interest in life. Seems as if there couldn't be anybody here like that. Look at this, in this light. But I presume it's here. It's one of the most genuine things in the world.

Young people take it two ways. Some of them decide to just have 'em — join something: join a church; join a Rotary Club; join something and have it over with. But there's always someone — (I've just been meeting them.) — there are always some around who stay in the pains of it.

I don't know whether I've got out of 'em myself yet, those pains. But I resolved, at some time along, not to have 'em if I didn't have 'em. You see, not to worry about it.

And it came to me this way, in a figure of speech, as so often. I thought to myself, I'll write a poem here and a poem there and a poem there. And they need have no connection; they need put together into no special great meaning, large meaning — no generalization. Never mind, they'll be like stars coming out at night, in the evening — one here, one there — all separate, you know, as it looks. And maybe, as the evening darkens, they'll constellate.

And they have, somewhat. Critics tell me now that they put together. That's some reward to me. It doesn't end it all, but it's quite a reward. [. . .]

But, you see, that's the kind of confidence — if I radiate anything — the kind of confidence in just waiting till this remark and that remark, this insight and that insight — (All separate; don't worry about 'em.) — as the time darkens, as your life darkens, they constellate; they make figures. And then you've got convictions. That's all of that.

All that's in the poems, too, that kind of interest. Not giving it up anywhere, that's the great bravery; just to wait, to give it time. Don't just give it up and climb in. Let it solve itself a lot. It's up to whom to solve it.

Then, when it comes to symbols in it all, I've been saying lately I've found myself in a kind of symbolism that I hadn't noticed all these years. I'm very fond of the symbol, apparently, of what might be the symbol of all symbols: the couplet, the rhymed couplet.

But that's a symbol, isn't it, of all — of all — all things like that; the way things come together? They separate and come together, separate and come together.

Someone says: "How about the amoeba? It seems very singular a creature." And I said: "Well, while you're looking at it, when it looks ever so single and one, it's probably troubled inside with becoming two. It needs a psychiatrist. It's beginning to divide."

All these things. Quips are like poems, you see. Little quips you make, like that, they're all toward this. They're all separate. Let 'em look ever so inconsistent, too.

Somebody introduced me in New York the other night as if I was all just made out of contradictions. That wouldn't worry me.

Let 'em, these things, look ever so different. Many a pair of things look like a standoff. You can't do anything with 'em; they just stand off. Well, let 'em stand off. What will come of it will.
[. . .]

Take the matter of a person like Brutus. You have Brutus in Shakespeare's play *Julius Caesar*, and you have him in Plutarch's *Lives*. And he's quite a nobility. He's the hero. He's the heroic republican that we only have a few of left. (He was getting pretty scarce then, too!)

There he is. He's a great figure in those two. And then most of you perhaps have read deep enough into Dante to know that

98

he's in the deepest hell, as one of the three worst people that ever lived — being mumbled forever in the mouth of a monster.

Now, what are you going to do with that? That's Shakespeare against Dante. Standoff!

I delight in 'em, I think. I like to leave 'em standing. Oh, you know, I'm like a dog that has a number of bones around, different parts of the yard. And he goes and gets one and worries it for a while. And then he covers it up a little and goes and worries another one.

I worry these different subjects, a little bit, now once in a while; get a poem out of 'em, you see — a poem here and a poem there and all that.

—at Dartmouth College, May 18, 1954:

THAT'S WHAT this man that I spoke of last night might say, that as we grow up we leave things behind. [. . .]

Again, to show what my convictions are, I always dislike people who are leaving everything behind them in that way. They were unfortunate I think, some of them, in reading bad books, just written for children, when they were young. And so they got over those, and they think that's the process all the way along, just the process of getting over things, to grow up.

If that's growing up, I don't want to grow up. I wouldn't want to.

Again, my convictions come in. I've got a dislike for that, that idea. I never got over liking any artist that I ever liked. He fell into a place among the others, but always what he was, if he was anything, stays with me. If he was nothing, it's different.

Something you live by
till you live by something else

In speaking at Amherst College on June 6, 1958, preliminary to his poetry reading that was a featured part of the institution's commencement weekend, Mr. Frost began reminiscently, making reference to Alexander Meiklejohn, philosopher and educational polemicist, who had served as Amherst's president from 1912 to 1924. The poet, now holding a lifetime appointment at the college as Simpson Lecturer in Literature, had earlier been a member of the Amherst faculty during three different intervals in the period 1917–38.

I REMEMBER the first time I ever spoke here. (I'm in a rather reminiscent mood this morning.) I was brought over here as a visitor by Mr. Meiklejohn in 1915 one morning. And I even remember what I talked about that morning and what trouble I got into for it.

I remarked, just offhand, that all the first best poetry is never set to music. I remarked that, and that brought several of the boys on me afterward. I remember their names even; we got to be great friends. I got acquainted that way, by saying something that wasn't exactly so, but came pretty near being so.

And I was offended the other day by something I saw in the paper about myself. It said, "Mr. Frost *holds* that all life is cellular." Holds! I "hold" nothing. And I wasn't *holding* that about poetry, exactly. I wouldn't call it a "tenet"; I'd call it a "tentative." That's something different.

And, yet, it's not a kind of academic thing that you put this way: "Wouldn't it be possible to take this position?" You see, just for the sake of argument. I always hate that, when boys say that to me. That used to be the fashion in the good old Meiklejohn days, to say, "Wouldn't it be possible to take this position?" Just for the row, you know. And I always said: "Do you *take* it — for life or death, you know? Do you mean it?" I suppress that.

But this other thing, this "tentative" thing, is something you live by till you live by something else. It's on the way. It's where you take a hitch — make a hitch there for the time being — something you live by.

Now, I was thinking this morning I'd say something about the Tower of Babel. I have said that "all life is cellular." [. . .] That's just an observation. That's nothing to live by, particularly, unless it's this: that there'll always be families; there'll always be countries. I needn't worry about there not being countries any more. Sometimes they try to scare me about it, that countries are all over and we're all going to be one world.

But this thing is something to lean on for the moment, anyway: that all life seems to be rather cellular, makes groups and things.

And I went on from that to think of the Tower of Babel, which is blamed for breaking us all up into nations. It reached so near the sky that heaven got worried about us and decided to scatter us into nations, so we wouldn't all come to heaven at once. Something like that; I suppose that's the story.

And now we have in New York — with the money of a very famous family — we have a "Tower of Anti-Babel," you might call it. It's going to undo what the Tower of Babel did. It's going to give us all one language, I suppose, make us all one world or one people.

That might make me anxious for the English Department, that I belong to; I'm a more or less faithful member of. But I think we must strengthen ourselves, as an English Department, so that when it comes to be one language in the whole world, it shall be English, not Volapuk or Esperanto or any ugly thing like that — and, most of all, that it shan't be Russian.

You know why? Because I don't want my poetry translated into Russian. I don't want to translate it into any language. I hope that the world will go on to be English and give my poetry a longer chance of staying untranslated. [. . .]

I'm going to read you some of the poems that I don't want translated. When I see them translated in other languages, I have just enough of those other languages to see how miserable they look. They really do, in all the places I've seen 'em. There's been a little, little glimmer somewhere.

I saw one little one in Spanish the other day, and I have enough Latin to do something with all those romance languages. I wouldn't want to say it to you, it was so ridiculous.

The reason is — if you stop and think of it, if you know language, if you care for language — the reason is that the idiom is what gets lost. The words come somewhere near, but even those are just approximations. And the idiom just goes entirely.

When I say one of my tentatives to a class, I like to say it so's to scare them. (I could well imagine I'm starting a class right now here.) At the beginning of the year, I like to say something that'd scare them so they'd want to hear what I was going to say the rest of the year — so they'd say: "Aw, that won't do. I'll go home and tell my mother on that." But they can't resist it. They keep following it, until toward the end of the year, they begin to say, "Oh, if he means it that way, it's all right — if he means it that way."

Means it. You see, it's the tone you take with it. Slowly the tone of what you say gets to people, so they know how you mean it to be taken. And the verse has the advantage of prose in that.

Something in verse carries a tone of extra meaning that makes it clearer and clearer, as you listen to it, as to how this is to be taken, this particular thing. That's the all-important thing about it. [. . .]

I often think that I've said things in poems, afterward, that were — long, long afterward — were indirectly answers to something that offended me in other people here. That conflict, you know; I hate direct conflict. (I wonder if that's lack of courage.) But I like to settle it somewhere, and it takes time. And sometime you get a phrase that's it, that's the answer to that.

For instance, I heard here on this platform once that the boys were shown — you were all shown — that there's no sharp line between good and evil. Evil isn't over here and good isn't here.

That had bothered me like fury, to hear that, because that is true that there isn't. But there's something there that's being left out. And long afterward, in a poem, I said, "There are roughly zones. . . ."32

There's no sharp line, but there's wavering lines — but "roughly zones" of good and evil. That satisfied me. But it took time for me to get to that.

It's in a poem. I was answering. And I often think that many a little line I slip in is my answer to something that I didn't settle way back.

Some girl said to me — granddaughter of mine, graduating from Smith, a year or two ago — she said to me, "Don't you think it's everybody's duty to do good in the world?" And I said, "I'd rather do well than good."

But she thought — (Wait till you hear.) — she thought a minute or two — (Sweet thing she is.) — and she said, "But wouldn't it be possible to do good well?"

It's a long time — (We see each other now and then.) — and

there's something to settle there. I let her have the field that day. She won, saying it would be possible "to do good well." But there's more to all that, isn't there?

For instance, all the ways of doing good are human. They're determined by the race, way back through the years. One way to do good is to be a doctor. Another way to do good is to be a preacher. Another way to do good is to be a teacher. Another good way is to be a plumber. You see, and go on.

I needn't go on. There are all sorts of ways. And those have all been found by the race.

And one of the ways is to do charity. That's what she's talking about. But to make that the only one of the ways to do good, you see, that's what I have to settle with her, still.

I've been thinking about it. She kept me thinking about it, that charity is one of the great appointed ways to do good. But to turn a government — (You see, now I'm getting political. I must stop that!) — to turn a government into just a charity institution would be a mistake, be as bad as turning us all into doctors, just making it all medical.

But all of these appointed ways are great. And I wouldn't take away from that as one great occupation, the charity work — and the department of charity.

Then, there's the department of justice, too, you know.

—at Wesleyan University, May 19, 1960:

To ME the greatest thing in the world is getting new answers. I think that's been my greatest interest in life, new answers. Sometimes they're just cute, and sometimes they're deep.

104

Some gamble – something of uncertainty

Mr. Frost's engagement at Boston University on October 30, 1958, was less than a week before the national biennial elections, and in his opening remarks he alluded to the fact that on the Massachusetts ballot that year there would be a referendum question pertaining to whether pari-mutuel betting on horse and dog racing would be allowed within the respective counties of the state.

I'VE BEEN TALKING various ways various places lately, and it just occurred to me tonight that I think you're all having to vote on an interesting subject here. I'm not, because I'm a Vermonter. But I believe you're all voting on the subject of gambling, aren't you? Is that going on here in Massachusetts?

Many thoughts about that, I've had. The common thought is that it's a minor evil that will go on, anyway, and you might as well profit by it. Now, that's low, isn't it?

But there is another strange thing that I've thought of many times: that if my life hadn't gamble in it, I would buy some gamble, the Irish Sweepstakes or something. Probably would — I don't know; I've never been without gamble, daily gamble.

You see, life is like that: love and need or love and desire, and enterprise and gamble. And the love should include desire, shouldn't it? And the enterprise should include gamble. And you shouldn't have to go outside for the desire or outside for the gamble — shouldn't have to. That's the high way of looking at it.

I sort of pity the people on the production line, who don't see what it's all about and have no gamble in their lives, unless it's in having an occasional riotous strike; something like that. And you can sympathize with it, the strike, because it introduces into their life something of uncertainty. They may get knocked on the head.

So, I just wanted to say that. And, now, in my poems, always along, I say things like this—in one line and pass over them, whether they get noticed or not. I say somewhere:

> But yield who will to their separation . . .

You see, the two things, separating the gamble from the enterprise.—

> . . . yield who will to their separation,
> My object in living is to unite
> My avocation and my vocation . . .

That is, the "vocation" is the regular part of it; the "avocation" is the irregular part of it, the gambler part of it. To unite them—

> As my two eyes make one in sight.
> Only where love and need are one,
> And the work is play for mortal stakes . . .

And I'm sure people have misunderstood that a lot, where I say, "And the work is play for mortal stakes." They think I mean the work is play. No, I mean the work is a gamble. You see? I want to put a hyphen into that; I should. The next time I print that I shall have it, "And the work is play-for-mortal-stakes." You see, the work is a gamble.—

> Is the work ever done . . .[33]

to any great purpose.

It's got to have that element in it. There must be uncertainty in it. And you can make what you please of that. You can make your religion out of that.

Somewhere else I say, " . . . something has to be left to God."[34] That's the part of life that is the most important of all: the gamble and the enterprise.

And I'm perfectly unscrupulous in saying that if I hadn't any enterprise at all that I can call an enterprise of my own, and there was no uncertainty in it, I'd buy some tickets in the Irish Sweepstakes, so I wouldn't know what might not happen to me anytime. I'd dedicate a certain amount of my miserable little bit to introducing some uncertainty into my dull life.

You do that about all things. Of course, you don't need to set any money on it at all. You go to games, and all you have to do is to set your heart on one side or the other, and win or lose with 'em. You go home defeated or victorious with the team. You get your uncertainty of an afternoon.

Some people work themselves all up. They get way up, a hope on one touchdown. And then they get way down on two touchdowns by the other side. And they scream and holler.

I'm more patient than that. In another poem I say, " . . . the strong are saying nothing until they see."[35] I wait till the last thing before I scream. But I'm the same uncertainty. I will have it.

—at Connecticut College for Women,
December 8, 1959:

ONE OF THE THINGS you're doing in poetry is bringing expression to a place where you never had it before. You know the expression and how the tone is to be taken, but it didn't belong quite in this place. You fetched it from some-where. You got it in church or in school or in a game or something. That's very important to me.

The future of the world

During 1958 Mr. Frost was named Consultant in Poetry at the Library of Congress — an appointment that would lead to his becoming, two years later, the library's Honorary Consultant in the Humanities. In the text that follows, from a presentation made at the University of Iowa on April 13, 1959 (less than three weeks after a gala observance in New York City of the poet's eighty-fifth birthday), he refers to meeting "some scientists pretty soon, in a big way," that being his intended participation in an international symposium on "The Future of Man," which was to be held at New York City in late-September 1959.

WHEREVER I GO they talk about me as if I was a wise guy, as if I had some sort of wisdom. And a young reporter in Washington the other day came to consult me about my wisdom — right like that. (I'm a consultant in the library down there for the year, just for the moment.) He said he wanted to ask me about the future of the world.

I said: "You want to know [. . .] about the future of the world? All right, I'll do the best I can.

"The future of the world. Well," I said, "hard as it is to tell about the past of the world" — (Everybody gets it different every time he writes a book, the Greeks and the Romans — and the Hittites; they must have been baseball players, I think! — and all that sort of thing.) — "hard as it is to get the past, it's harder to get the future.

"But listen," I said, "the future is going to be much the same as the present" — (This is me telling him.) — "for a long, long time, and maybe to end with.

"You see, there have been evolutionary changes, all down the ages, that we are the tip-front of. But many branches of the evolutionary thing have just come to nothing. They've died out. And I think our tip is about to die out; the next hundred thousand years or so. But it's not going any further. There's never going to be any superman," I told him. You see, never.

Now it's me talking. And then I said: "You know, this is the analogy: When a man gets so that he's thoroughly self-conscious, his growth stops. And we are the self-consciousness of creation."

That scare you? We are the self-consciousness of creation. Creation has reached its self-consciousness in us. And that means we're going to fold out, spread out, and all that. But this is a dead end — hundred thousand years from now. (I just don't set the date. I'm cautious about that.) And that's good.

I'm going to meet some scientists pretty soon, in a big way, who are interested in us this way. I say reached a point of high self-consciousness, which is completion. But they say that we've reached a point where we can take our own evolution in hand and make ourselves anything we please. (And that's amusing, too, their prediction against my prediction.)

I said, "Don't believe 'em." — I told this fellow, this newspaperman. And he went off and reported that I'd nominated Kennedy for President. You never know what a newspaperman will get out of it! I hadn't mentioned Kennedy then. But that's what he got out of it.

The beautiful thing — just to linger a minute longer — I told him the beautiful thing about that is that science may talk as it pleases — (And it is the greatest enterprise of all enterprises.) — but whose enterprise is it? It's ours.

And what's the best statement of who we are? It's man's enterprise, and what's the best statement of what man is? The best statement of what man is is all the literature, all the music, all the humanities of the past. It's a very, very enormous thing, a very great thing.

It's slowly realized in life but that man is the owner and manager and director of science. That makes the reconciliation with science and the humanities.

Humanities is an attempt, anyway, to describe the man whose enterprise is science. Get that. The history of the world describes the man whose enterprise science is.

It's our enterprise. Very grand thing; all for it, we all are, the enterprise. But it doesn't mean that that enterprise will ever tell you anything about our personal relations with each other, our passions and our loves and hates and all that. That will never be touched by science.

That's us; that's man. And he is the owner and swayer and manager, altogether, of science. And there's no antagonism at all. Heroism and glory and all are in this enterprise of ours, clear into anywhere you want to go.

I'm in a position to tease the scientists about what they are talking about doing, but haven't done yet. I think it's a great joke. Here we are; you'd think we were in the moon tomorrow.

A friend of mine, talking to me on the telephone from England, said he was in favor of stopping science. And I said to him, "But you're not in favor of stopping literature, even when it's a little pornographic."

He said, "You have me there." And I said: "What do you want to stop science for? It's our science. It's our greatness." And he said: "Well, I don't want the moon spoiled. That's for lovers."

That's sentimental talk, you see. But wherever we go, we'll be earthlings going — earthlings — and we'd better take our lunch with us. [. . .]

You have to think that all over. You have to think about who has the best description of what we are. Who? It's too big to talk about: all the great drama, the great poems, the great songs, the great histories. Thucydides; everybody's in it, you know, with their great history like that. Herodotus is in it. And what *are* we?

Now, you can't believe that any extempore talker like me or any extempore psychiatrist or psychologist can give you a better description of what we are than that vast book of the past, the book of the worthies and unworthies. [. . .]

And then I turn from that. My poetry is only a little contribution to that book of the worthies and unworthies — what they call the "wisdom," all the vast wisdom of it all — that is the description of us, the statement of us, of man.

And when you wonder what the humanities are, that's what they pretend to be — anyway, what they undertake to be — to cover that: all the poetry in prose and verse of many languages; prose and verse, mind you. And religion — with the Bible; the strange wisdom that's scattered through the Bible and all that — that's got to do with it.

— at Dartmouth College, May 13, 1952:

PERHAPS I ought to say that the more dangerous a thing is, the more beautiful it is. Everything beautiful, that's truly beautiful, is dangerous.

.   .   .

ALL there is to your life and mine is mixing with everybody. That's all, in the give and take. And as soon as that gets discovered and there's too much give on one hand and too much take on the other — as between a professor and his class it can be, it could be, it might be (It's always the fear of the professor with his class, that it's too much give on his end and too much take on their end.) — that's a disorder.

Hang around for
the refinement of sentiment

On November 17, 1959, Mr. Frost spoke at Rockhurst College, as part of the institution's fiftieth-anniversary celebration, and received the college's Chancellor Award. During this same interval at Kansas City, Missouri, the poet made a visit to the headquarters of Hallmark Cards Incorporated.

THIS IS GREAT pleasure being in the middle of the United States with this crowd. Isn't it something? I feel as if every year I got nearer the center of the United States, in a metaphorical way. But here I am literally at the middle of the United States, with plenty of the United States here with me. [. . .]

I'm a teacher more than I am a farmer, but I've been both all the way along. And I've been a newspaperman, too. I've been — you know, American style — I've been a little of everything as I came up with an art — with an art, you see.

And one of the things about art is that you have to find a refuge, while you're starting it, from hasty judgments. And farming was one for me. And teaching was another. And newspaper work was another. The years of hasty judgment I got by that way.

I wonder sometimes if anything can be done about that, to make it easier; foundations and things, if they can help — if they could find an underground cave for poets and artists to get into, against bombs, as well as hasty judgments.

You realize that I'm not judging the judges. I'm one of the judges of others, and troubled in myself all the time about the new boys coming up; how to single out those that are fit to bet on. And that is a hard part of the world, part of art and all.

The United States is more concerned about it than any country in the world, probably, unless it's Russia. I don't know, they seem to be working hard, too.

School is a fine thing. You can linger in school. I didn't linger; I ran out. If I'd known enough, I would have seen that it was a fine place to hide in and a comfortable place — and a place that made it comfortable for my friends and relatives. They could say: "He's at So-and-So. He's at Columbia."

As it was, as I lived it, they didn't know what to say about me. They didn't say, "He was failing as a poet." That didn't come out. It didn't get that bad. But "he" was nothing you wanted to talk about. Those are serious things.

Now, the education. I've been quoted as saying, "Education is hanging round till you catch on."[36] That sounds rather slangy, and it is meant to be. But it describes the whole thing, "hanging round till you catch on"; that is, you hang around for the refinement of sentiment about all these things: success and failure, life and death, and religion, politics.

That's the all-important part of it. You might as well learn two or three subjects while you're about it, too. And that keeps you from getting too self-conscious about it all. Get busy. But the busyness isn't the main thing — being with the right people till you get the right sentiment about many things.

Precepts don't do it. They help a little. And there's no teacher does as much to you as some of your fellows who just exchange glances over something foolish you say. That punishes you and that puts you in, whips you in, and teaches you about sentiment.

Sentiment is a very hard thing to talk about, and a very hard thing to practice without running into sentimentality. You're always dancing on that dangerous verge of sentimentality. And the great masters of sentiment are the great artists, that's all. And that is school, too, you know. The school should be a place of the great arts, the humanities.

113

Our schools more and more — in the last fifty years that I've known them and taken part in them — have been more and more like what I describe. I'm not complaining. I'm not advocating. I'm describing what they are. [. . .]

I've been — speaking today — I've been in a place where sentiments are handled for birthdays, Christmas, and all sorts of cards. And very interesting to me to see the people at work in there, making sentiments or writing out sentiments, and pictures to go with them — and people of various nationality at work on it. And I looked seriously at 'em, the young people at the work, and I thought a great many thoughts.

For instance, they probably didn't have any card — (I suppose they didn't. I didn't ask that.)—about the death of Christ — (You see, that's one of the mighty sentiments.) — and the great sentiment about failure, defeat, and the need of mercy. Those aren't Christmas cards.

The Christmas card is more like: "God rest ye noble gentlemen, / Know you no dismay, / For Jesus Christ, our Saviour, / Was born on Christmas day." You know, cheerful about His life; looking at Him as a saviour of us, by what He went through. But that's a sentiment *very* difficult to handle — dark, deep sentiment. [. . .]

Some sentiments of my books are tender things. Tenderness is another difficult thing to handle. And sometimes you wouldn't expect to have it brought out in a crowd like this. And sometimes you wouldn't expect to see it in a newspaper. You'd think they'd get to something tragic or dramatic or something like that. But tender and the gentle you hesitate about.

I've often hesitated. I have certain poems that I've never brought out onto my sleeve, so to speak. They're there in the book, and I'd rather people would encounter them in the book than encounter them with me in public; quite a few of 'em.

114

People ask me if I don't like those. Why do I avoid 'em all the time? It's 'cause I like 'em too well, the ones I'm sensitive about.

But that's one of the great questions in my life. How public is my life? It didn't begin very publicly, you can be sure. I didn't have to be afraid of having anybody laugh at me. They didn't know I was there; that was all.

If they had noticed me, they might have tapped their heads, you know. I've known fellows who suffered the cruelty of being thought of as just a village defective — poets. I knew one through many years. [. . .]

But the education. I'm always getting a new definition of education. It's an old one, "hanging round till you catch on." I made that last year. And this one is that it's the refinement of sentiment. It's getting you to refine your sentiments and handle your sentiments with refinement.

And the masters of sentiment are the great poets, the great dramatists, the great novelists, too.

—at Hebrew Union College, April 2, 1960:

THE PROPHET and the poet seem to me to go together, somewhat. The prophet is the great bewarer. Bewareness is his life, telling the king what to beware.

And the poet, his great thing is awareness — awareness, luxuriating in what God gives us; luxuriating in it all, the spiritual, the mental, the physical.

—Yale University, November 6, 1962:

THERE ARE two kinds of music, the music of poetry and the music of music, and they aren't the same thing.

What I think I'm doing
when I write a poem

This excerpt is from Mr. Frost's January 19, 1960, talk and reading before a Dartmouth College audience.

SOMETIMES I WONDER if I wouldn't talk a little about just what a poem is for me, what I think I'm doing when I write a poem. "What do you think you're doing?" we say, you know. I never really dealt with that. [. . .]

But it is sort of an interesting question. What do you think you're doing in television when they tell you to come walking down a lane talking to yourself? Don't they know that the soliloquy's gone out of fashion?

They don't seem to. They had me at a graveyard the other day, a famous graveyard, at Newport, Rhode Island, and asked me to walk around talking to myself about the stones. [. . .]

But what does one think he's doing? They might say: "You write a poem when you're alone, don't you? Are you soliloquizing then?"

Well, that's a hard one. You're talking to someone. And it's a long-developed convention that you sit there by yourself. You can't do it with anybody in the room.

And I can't do it aloud. If I did it aloud it would spoil it. It's as I hear it in my mind's ear that it's at its best. I can't quite say out loud to you here the way I hear the poem in my mind's ear.

I've heard actors and actresses — a few, a very few — who got such an exquisite reproduction of the tone of voice meant in a sentence of writing that I worshipped 'em. That's something

116

that's followed me all my life. I've gone to hear the great ones — to see that their difference is just that, something exquisitely close to the truth of the tone that's intended. And there is something there that is to be caught, you know. You don't just make it any way you please.

When Horatio says — (Someone asks him if he believes in all this superstition about what the rooster does at certain hours of the night.) — he just says, "So I have heard, and do in part believe. . . ."[37] Oh, isn't that a great sentence, in my sense of the word? [. . .] A very gentleman's answer to all these things. It's the answer that I bring into mind whenever there's something I don't quite get, you know, about things.

I met somebody the other day that I talked with witches about. He was ten years in a concentration camp. But he came originally from Poland, where he said it was quite the familiar thing to have witch women around.

We have transmediums, and I find so very few people ever saw one. I've seen 'em — never consulted 'em; but I know what's going on there, somewhat.

And when they say, "There is something extrasensory; there are things beyond." I say, "So I have heard, and do in part believe. . . ." (I don't say I don't know what part.)

And there's a nice distinction there. That's not liberality; that's sheer worldliness, you see. I'm that worldly. That's what Horatio was, just worldly. He wasn't a liberal, just worldly. He'd risk your thinking that, if you'd risk his thinking something else. Just we won't make a to-do about anything. [. . .]

I'd often think a poem might have this for its little preface. It might be, "How would it be to put it this way?" You see? "How would it be to put it this way?" — whatever it's going to be. And then the end would be, "Do you get it?" That's in it all the time. But you don't ever say 'em.

You say something sort of wicked and a little perverse and as much as you can do, you know — as you can get away with. See? The poem is getting away with something. You're getting away with something.

And your humor and your mood. Sometimes it goes very deep and dark. And it goes very cheerful. And it goes oftentimes very wicked, teasing and wicked. That's in it.

Now, this controversy that's going on — (I don't read literary magazines, and I don't read reviews. But they come to me on the air. People tell me things.) — I know there's something going on there, about obscurity and making difficulty.

And I know some of my friends, I just wish they wouldn't throw themselves away, so fashion — just be obscure and think they've done something because nobody knows what they're talking about. They invoke the past, somebody that didn't get read very much in his lifetime. But that isn't the point at all. That's some accidence of neglect.

You take Emily Dickinson. Lots of the little poems, if they'd got out, they would have got round. They didn't happen to get out. She courted interest. She courted it. She wrote to the right people sometimes. But they didn't get waked up to an interest in her. She'd say a tragic thing like this:

> The heart asks pleasure first,
> And then, excuse from pain;
> And then, those little anodynes
> That deaden suffering;
>
> And then, to go to sleep;
> And then, if it should be
> The will of the Inquisitor,
> The liberty to die.[38]

That kicked around a long time — very deadly sentiment; deep, dark one. [. . .]

And we aren't writing poetry to forget darkness. It's a blended thing. It isn't all Christmas cards and birthday cards. It's something deep, deep and dark oftentimes.

And you ask people to "come on in." It's like that when you write a poem. Come on in; share my mood; take it with me. And sometimes it's one way and sometimes it's another.

That's the first thing to say. And, then, every poem, for me, is a little feat of association, putting a couple of things together, as you do in a quip or a witticism or a thing. A poem has got that. That's the core of the poem.

You see, the point of her poem — that one that I said — it hits its high place when she calls it "The will of the Inquisitor." You see what she's after and who she's calling "the Inquisitor." If you aren't in on it, you're out. That's all.

And it's a partly, a percentage thing. Some people get you in one mood, and some will get you in another. Some don't go with you in that sentiment. And if it gets shallow and political and you talk partisan, about forty-eight percent will be on your side and the other fifty-two against you — or vice-versa, as you're a Democrat or a Republican.

We aren't playing at that level — exactly. Once in a while, sometimes you get a little political. And you can tell with your audience that you're getting on dangerous ground that way.

Now, all thought — all thought — in philosophy, in science, in poetry is a feat of association. Just put it this way: being reminded by the sight of this that's happening, that's in front of you, by something you'd almost thought you'd forgotten — in a book or in life or somewhere — bringing things together.

And all the great achievements in science are just feats of association. Now, the little poem may be a very slight one, a little

119

feat of association — just the same as a joke may be a very slight one; may be a rather deep one or it may be a very slight one.

Some saying, some country saying, often looks more or less humorous. And when you think of it, it's very, very deep; comes out of great depths of association, putting this and that together — as we say, "two and two together." [. . .]

One of my favorite occupations for years — one of my favorite pleasures and times of sense of success — is when I made a good couplet in a poem, within the poem, or out all by itself. I have a few around. You may have seen them, and you may not. [. . .]

The couplet — the rhyming, the putting things together by rhyme — I heard described as the degeneracy of poetry that came in after Latin went out. (I read that in a book not terribly long ago.) And, you know, it's just to misunderstand the rhyme. The rhyme is an outward symbol of this inner coupling that I'm talking about — putting this and that together — this feat of coupling. It's an outer symbol of it. (Talking symbol in these days.)

It has that same sort of thing, bringing this and that together — more on the surface, more in the form of the thing than in the soul of the thing, the spirit of the thing. That's my "How would it be to put it that way?" You see, "Do you get it?" [. . .]

You'll notice, as you come through a poem, where I'm having a very good time. You can tell I'm having a very good time, because — more than usual, that is — what you like to call the "inspiration" is good. You feel you're up; that I'm having some good couplets.

Sometimes they're separated by others, you know. There'll be four: A rhyming with C, and B rhyming with D; that kind of thing. But it's still something of the way they clink — clink, you know — the way, click and come.

That's what I think I'm doing. I'm only telling you what I think I'm doing.

These fellows, I just wonder about 'em. Some of them friends of mine, but I wonder how they have the courage just to write on the principle, I think — (I'm only guessing at their principle.) — that an arrangement is all there is to it. So, why not arrange nothing? It's just as interesting to arrange nothing as it is something. And that's what's the matter. They're arranging nothing.

They've got some idea, I'm afraid, that to use a word that surprises you by coming in at all, because it doesn't belong in, that's a feat. I don't know what they are up to unless that. [. . .]

About nothing? No, it's going to be about something with me. One of my great friends, a poet — (Gone to his reward; whatever that is.) — he said to me one night when he had been drinking a little too much, he said, "The trouble with you is you write on subjects." And I said to him, "The trouble with you is ——" (I imitated his manner.) I said, "The trouble with you is you write on bric-a-brac."

I didn't think he took that in. He was in this state of mind. But the next book he sent me, he'd written in it — s-m-o-r-e; s'more — "s'more bric-a-brac."

And we were at variance a little, as friends. As a matter of fact, we should have known each other earlier than we did. We were a little off, just because of the difference. It kept us away from each other.

That's a curious thing, how protective that is. I don't live in the crowd so I live with people of whom they say, "He's a fine fellow, but he can't write." I never stay with people I feel that way. I don't have to, because I live in the country. But some of 'em live with each other and say that magnanimous thing all the time about each other: "He's a great fellow, but I can't read him." That's supposed to be the big style.

I don't like to be thrown with anybody who, primarily, I don't like for his work. That's a dear thing to him, and why should I pretend to like him, when I think he's a rotten writer?

And I have strained a point now and then — to go to these difficult people — I've strained a point, when I'm thrown with 'em by accident, to *try* to like the awful stuff. And I've been a little insincere, a little false about it.

And when they got mad at me for some reason — my religion or my politics or something — I was greatly relieved, because I didn't have to pretend to like their poetry anymore.

I'm not honest, but I wish I were. You see, I aspire to be honest. [. . .]

I'm going to have to award a thousand dollars to a western poet tomorrow night or the night after — day after tomorrow — at the Poetry Society of America, won by a fellow who lives in Denver.

I know who he is. I just found that out. I never saw the poem. I don't know what the poem's like. But it's a narrative poem. The prize is a thousand dollars for an American narrative poem.

I asked somebody who'd seen it, "Is it in free verse?" And he said, "I'm afraid it is." You see, he knows that bothers me a little. But it doesn't too much, again. I'd rather it'd be in some sort of measure, beat. I want to start the metronome when it goes.

Now, I haven't been talking footnotes at all or defending myself at all. That isn't a defense. I could be entirely wrong.

I was just telling you, when people might ask me from the audience — (Many times I bet they've wanted to ask me.) — "What do you think you're doing, when you write a poem? What do you think you're doing?"——

I've had a newspaperman say to me, "Why do you write verse at all, when there's honest prose to write?"

Why do you? Why do you sing at all? Why do you dance? Why do you beat time? Why do you drum? And so on.

It's an old convention. I don't suppose I would have written poems at all if somebody else hadn't written some. I wouldn't have started a thing like that, not if you come right down to it.

—at the University of Delaware, May 16, 1959:

WHEN I'm reading longer poems, some of the long poems, if you were very discerning and if you were very penetrating, you could see that I take almost too much pleasure where I'm having great luck with the couplets.

They can get very mechanical, of course, and so much a matter of mere virtuosity that you wonder how great a poet Pope was. And there's always that danger of poetry, of getting to be a virtuoso, anyway; that is, a person who can do it all on his know-how, without having any spirit in it. [. . .]

But, you see, there's something more, isn't there? The poem has got to have that, the feat of association. And then it's got to have the couplets, the forms of doubleness. And then it's got to be flushed with something. And I know very well that I hide that from myself sometimes some: that it must be flushed, like color to the cheek, something of human feeling, something of sympathy, something that's near — that I don't like to talk about technically; it isn't a technical thing. [. . .]

This doubleness goes on all the time, more or less. People conscious of it often speak of it. With me — a good deal of it, the ulteriority — I used to say I had an "ulteriority complex"; that I always was — (Always, sure; I agreed.) — I was always thinking of more than I was saying. But if I'd wanted to say it, I'd have said it out. You see, I want to keep something back.

123

Of the "elect" and the "elected"

Part of the context for what Mr. Frost said at Phillips Exeter Academy on October 23, 1960, was the presidential-election campaign then being waged between Senator John F. Kennedy, the Democratic nominee, and the Republican candidate, Vice President Richard M. Nixon.

I WAS THINKING of a word tonight, just one word: the word "elect." And in this neighborhood — not far from here, down in Salem and so on — it once meant something very different from what it means now. These two men that you're watching on the television every night — (I suppose it's almost every night.) — of these two men one will be "elected." And that's a little different from being "elect."

"Elect" is almost like the word "select." There was a man named Calvin, in Geneva, who fixed it on everybody — on his Protestant world, on Geneva and on Scotland — that only a few were elect. Of all those born, only a few were elect.

You can pick that up — if you want verse for it — you can pick it up in the Bible. You can pick almost anything up in the Bible. That's why some people don't believe in the common people reading the Bible. They don't know how to handle it.

In the Bible it says that people that aren't elect can't read poetry. Many people will try to act as if they were reading poetry, of course. But only a few are reading it, the Bible says. Many people will act as if they were religious, but only a few will be saved.

Dreadful, isn't it? And then you look at each other — (Right now you look, and there's someone beside you.) — and you think:

"I wonder if you're saved. I wonder if you can read poetry. I wonder if you know a joke when you hear one."

It's only the elect can take a joke, too, you see. And there's quite a difference there. Take a joke like this, for instance. Suppose I were giving you an oral examination now, and I tell you one like this. (All of you can laugh, if you want to, but I can tell which are laughing honestly. We used to say, "like a duck" I can.) There was a man dreamt all night he was eating a twenty-pound marshmallow. All night dreamed that, and in the morning he couldn't find his pillow. (I wish I had made that up!)

And, you know, what you're getting an education for is so that you'll wish you thought of some things first, before others did. That's to prove you are one of the elect, I tell you. An envy is a good thing to develop, envy of those that are first to think and first to say and first to be.

And that brings you to the wonderful question of leadership. I've heard a lot around colleges about being trained for leadership. But I suspect that it's only the elect that have it. The rest have to behave.

The old saying: "You can't be like us. You must try to be as like us as you can." That's what the elect say. You see, they know they're elect. But the thing that spoils all that is that no man on earth can judge another man very well about that. That's too fine.

My people, I know, were here in New England and were of those that didn't bother to feel elect. They were very worldly, the ones that came here first for me. But the ones that ruled the colony and all that, had to be pretty sure they were elect. They weren't voted for. They had to just come to that feeling, that they were elect.

Want to hear something that sounds very undemocratic, right out of the Bible? It says, "These things are said in poetry ——" (In "parable" is another word for it.) "These things are said in

125

parable, so the wrong people won't understand them and so get saved."[39]

That sounds like another joke, doesn't it? And it is, kind of. At least it's very undemocratic, isn't it? But it's very aristocratic. It's very Calvinistic in psychology. And we laugh, we sneer, we dismiss the story of Calvin and his tyranny over Geneva, his tyranny over Scotland — all based on this idea.

And what he said was, virtually, that a few people are elect and are what you might call "sincere," and they're saved. And the rest of 'em have to be hypocrites and pretend they're saved — all the rest of 'em. And they had to obey the police. And they had to obey the preacher. And they had to take their medicine — the koine. [. . .]

Now, you see, this question; we have to dismiss it. It's all over, all over our talk. It all comes to the word "sincerity," I suppose, nowadays. We say one person seems "sincere" about art, we'll say — talking about paintings. And some people are really insincere. They keep up an appearance. They think travel is broadening, and they travel. And they go to the museums, and they do the best they can.

But who's to decide? Nobody else can decide. I couldn't, marking you in school. Yes, I could! I could, in a way. In classes I know in the course of a year, even without asking any questions, about who's "A," "B," "C" — and "out"; those are outside of it.

And sometimes I think that some of the teachers I could judge that way. I judge 'em about my own poetry. They make some awful breaks, from my point of view, some of them do. And some of 'em are just as easily right as if I had brought 'em up. Isn't that strange?

We live with each other in this state of judging sincerity. We're drawn to those that we feel drawn, and sort of averse to those that we feel are not "in"; not to the manor — *manor* — born. (That word you have to be very careful of. It sounds as if I may be saying "m-a-n-n-e-r." But I'm not. It's another word. It's spelled another way: to the "manor" born.) [. . .]

Take a matter of patriotism, again, sincere patriotism. Sometimes you'd say, wouldn't you, that the quiet people about it — that aren't whooping it all the time and aren't hunting communists all the time and doing all that sort of thing — are probably nearer the elect, nearer the chosen spirits?

But perhaps it's this way. Some seem elect in one of the arts — one in music, another in another. We've got nothing to go on here. We have to live together, elect and non-elect — and looking suspiciously at each other, you know, and thinking, "You, you poor thing, you're out; you're going to burn in hell." And so on.

One of the great cardinals of England, Manning, had it come over him that the whole thing lay in one place in the Bible. It says — (I think I can come somewhere near it.) — "but the terrible and unbelieving" — not "terribly unbelieving" — "but the terrible and unbelieving shall partake of the fire of brimstone that burns forever."[40] (I've missed it a little. But that's somewhere near it.)

And he said, from the age of eight, all through his life, that was the most governing thought in his life — and what it meant to be believing and what it meant to be unterrible. (I don't know what that means.) You see: "the terrible and unbelieving shall partake of the fire of brimstone."

It governed him all his life. It came over him, the first terrible moment, when he was about eight years old, and he got under a table to protect himself. And he said it never left him, that thought, the rest of his life: Was he a true person? [. . .]

I've never talked about it to anybody this way, as severely as this, before. Here's a whole lot of you, and are you "in"? Are you

127

taking this in the right way? Are you taking this "culture," as they call it, in the right way? Or are you taking it in the way that Sinclair Lewis would make fun of?

What a mean man he was. He spent his time just being mean about the non-elect. That's right; that's right. I thought of it the other day. In a book of humor — humorous stories — there was one of his that wasn't funny a bit. It was just mean, mean about the non-elect. [. . .]

But it matters in a way — (In a sort of a free way; you mustn't be too strict about it.) — but it matters not to "feign emotion" — (Stevenson says, Robert Louis Stevenson, never to "feign emotion."[41]) — never to feign delight; never to pretend you're in on anything that you're not in on.

And it's a fine mental age to stay in, that lives in a kind of fear of that, awe of it.

Now, take me and Shelley. I have never pretended I liked him. I remember he was given to me when I was fourteen years old, a book. And I went to work on him; and I gave him up. And then — (My mental age is sort of permanent about that.) — I was afraid I was to blame. So, I read him again in about a year or two or three or four or five. (You see, I didn't have to hurry. I wasn't in any class.) And so on, down to now. And, no.

'Twas the other way with Keats. I was given a book about the same time. And I turned away from that — on Keats' own showing. Keats says — in a little preface to the first poem in the book *Endymion* — he calls it "mawkish." And it certainly was. And I felt the mawkishness. And I dared to dislike him.

And then by accidence, you know, I took another time, for fear it was my fault. And this time I didn't begin at the beginning of the book again. (I've learned never to begin with a poet's first poem. Plunge in somewhere else. Stick a pin in, the way they used to do with the Bible, and see what you get.) And then I came on the odes of the greatest poet since Shakespeare.

128

But now I'm bothered with the "Beatniks." I've dismissed them two or three times. But I'm still afraid that it might be my fault. So, we'll look again.

But this thing: Are you "in"? Are you "in"; have you got it? It's the same question with a pitcher. You watch the great pitchers, the great ones that have something special. And how much can it be used? How many times a week?

There was a fellow named "Iron Man" McGinnity that pitched five and six days a week. And nobody is asked to do that anymore; that is, the spirit fails. There wouldn't be that much spirit in anyone. This is the thing we're talking about. How much of this real quality can be called on? [. . .]

Take these two people running for the presidency. You're probably partisan about 'em. I'm not. I'm a Democrat, but — (Wait till you hear the rest of it.) — I've been more or less unhappy since 1896.

You see, "election"; isn't it a strange word? The "elected" and the "elect" — two different words, really. The same thing, really, only one's elect of God, chosen of God, and the other's chosen of the mob rule in America. [. . .]

Speaking of "leadership" again; how do we get it? First comes impulse. That's young; comes out of youth, in that sense — impulse: falling in love, being brave, charging into life, games and war and everything. The charge is young. That's the leadership there is there.

Shakespeare speaks of having taught a horse to be managed that's got to be managed. And out of that comes some that are elect — somebody elect — to take charge of all that impulse and give it leadership. It comes out of the mob. You don't know how.

And if you're like me — if you've been watching these two people running for office — I don't know how you felt about it, but all the time I felt, I wish they were a little bit more impetuous, that they took a lead the same as Franklin Roosevelt would or the way Teddy Roosevelt would. (It seems to run in the Roosevelt family, going back there, doesn't it?)

Something of that sort of seizing the thing and carrying it; they don't seem to seize it. They haven't got that fierceness about it. Maybe they're too young. But they haven't that strength, to me. I want more, anyway.

I wish for them — (I'm not talking against them.) — I just wish they had more of that. I look in vain. Maybe you can't do it on a television. Maybe it's too much of a Hollywood affair. I don't know what's the matter with it — disappointment.

—at Amherst College, April 25, 1960:

BEFORE YOU give God up, you'd better know a whole lot about the word "grace." It has a remarkable history. [. . .]

There are two words the Puritans talked about, "justification" and "sanctification." [. . .] They were great words that they worked on. [. . .] By the "sanctification" they meant this same thing, "grace."

Poetry ought to mean that on all our learning. It ought to mean that on the humanities. Poetry is sort of the grace of humanities.

This justification/sanctification: "Justification" means "works," you know; and that saves you by "works"— doing good and doing right and studying hard and all that. And the "sanctification" is sort of almost mysterious — the grace of God; and if you got it, you're saved; if you aren't, no matter how hard you work, you're damned. And the word "grace" comes in in sanctification.

Fall in love at sight

Less than a week before the 1960 election day that would draw the Kennedy/Nixon presidential contest to its close, Mr. Frost, in Los Angeles, met on the morning of November third with members of the student body at Occidental College. In beginning his remarks, he quoted from a recent exchange of comments between himself and Alexander Meiklejohn, former president of Amherst College.

You can't be having a time like this campaign without thinking about democracy, where it came from and what it is. I'm going to talk about that later. But you can't be educated as much as you can, unless you're just born to be a rank insider, without wondering what education is all about. Some people just become technical in their education, and then they're lost inside of it.

I heard the famous Mr. Meiklejohn of California, and Massachusetts, too — the famous disturber — say the other day that he's writing a book on law, because the lawyers don't know anything about law. I said, "You mean they're technical insiders?" He said, "That's what's the matter with 'em, insiders."

Suppose I said to you, "What are you getting an education for?" Some of you would just say you're getting it because other people get it, all that can. But I'm going to tell you what you're getting it for, in a word.

You're getting it so that you can come somewhere near falling right when you fall in love at sight — whether with a poem, with an ambition, with a party, a cause, or a hero — when you get to that age of falling.

I think particularly of poems. The only good reader is the

131

reader who has got where he can safely read at sight and fall in love at sight.

Now, I don't have to enlarge on that too much. But let me tell you that that can go very wrong. Your family are behind this, as well as the school. Everything's behind it, this moment when you fall in love at sight, with whatever it is, a cause or a girl or whatever it is.

Your family's so much interested in it that they often are distressed at the moment when you fall. And they want to do something about it. But it's too late.

That breaks up families, breaks ties and all that. And a lot of 'em don't know enough to know that, that it's too late. It's what's gone before in the education and in the family life.

And the education is like this. It's sometimes a drudgery of life, a drudgery of living along — trial and error with all sorts of things. What's the right thing to do? And what's the right thing to say? And you get that from the expression on the faces of your companions, how they take what you say. You can tell whether you've made a hit or haven't made a hit. And slowly that's getting you to know all about the people you've got among and belong among.

Let's put it this way. You get among the books, among the paintings, among the compositions, the music. You have got to get so you know how to take 'em and say the right thing about 'em and *do* the right thing about 'em. And you're watching everybody around you, teachers and all. The teachers have a lot to say about it. You've got to try to please them a little, you know, to get "A."

But all that's just part of it. Let me take the poems. You read A — at any time in your life and any kind of poem. It's poem A. You read that the better to read B. You read that the better to read C. You read that the better to read D. The better that to read A.

You see, this isn't a continuous progress, it's a circulation. You're getting among the people; you're getting among the poems. They throw light on each other.

You develop into somebody that can be trusted to fall in love at sight, with a cause or a girl. That's what you're at college for. It's just a part of all that.

My personal history is of eight or ten times in my life when I came across a poem or a picture — poem particularly, I can remember — when I was swept away; when it came over me, came over me and I was swept away.

I could be wrong. That's the adventure of life — the adventure of life, falling in love at sight. [. . .]

I saw an advertisement — just to talk a moment longer — a write-up about the school of technology in Boston, which is of course a rival of what you have here at Pasadena. It said right out — (I wonder who wrote it.) — that it was changing life; it was a great machine grinding away there, and fifty years from now we wouldn't be the way we are now at all.

Am I prepared to take that? Yeah, I think so. What will be changed? I can even generalize on what will be changed and what *won't* be changed.

The education won't be changed, in this way. You'll still be anxious to say the right thing and do the right thing at the moments of contact with poetry and people and things. You'll still be in that predicament, to live among people, live among books, live among paintings, and so on. That'll still be the problem. [. . .]

Well, now, the theme is — (You see, I'm still lingering on it a little.) — the theme is what you are old enough to read at sight is your happiest guide in the world; know how to take it at sight, without study.

The study, yes. Oh, that goes on some all around, the drudgery and the study. But you can't study yourself. Sometimes the thing that you know already and is in your head, you haven't really seen. Where Shakespeare says, for instance:

> It is the star to every wandering bark,
> Whose worth's unknown, although its height
> be taken.[5]

Now, he's talking about love, but he means the North Star. His figure is the North Star, "Whose worth's unknown, although its height be taken."

Now, I probably said that for years, in my head, and liked it in a way. But all of a sudden something dawned on me about it. And this dawn is, again, a moment of falling in love at sight. That's a beautiful line. [. . .]

Now I'll say some of my own poems to you. And if you know how to take poetry, you'll always think of what I say about the extravagances of it. It's one of the figures that belongs to it. Be carried away; the poem that comes over you with a rush and you go.

And that's so with everything. It may be athletics that comes over you that way. It may be a profession. It's something that you can't help doing. That's, again, what I mean; there's another way to put that.

Don't ever get married, I might tell you, unless you can't help it, unless you're carried away. Unless you're carried away; that's all of life.

—at New York University, March 23, 1956:

"GROWTH" is a much more important word than "evolution." It's the whole business really, growth.

Thinking about generalizations

In this extract from a talk and reading at Dartmouth College on November 29, 1960, Mr. Frost alludes to a visit he was soon to have from "some Russians," and in doing so makes observations that might be taken as constituting something of a prelude to parts of the conversation he would have less than two years later with Premier Nikita Khrushchev, during the poet's "goodwill mission" to the Soviet Union, undertaken under the auspices of the U. S. Department of State. He also refers herein to the visit that he had made to England during the spring of 1957.

I WAS JUST thinking about generalizations. [. . .] I like to tell all young people — (I was thinking I would.) — that they mustn't say, when a person makes a good generalization, "That's too simple." — and spoil all their generalizations. If you don't want them to think, stop their generalizing.

Now, every poem I write, I think must be a kind of generalization. It's got one in it somewhere, you can be pretty sure. You want to look out.

For instance, I say very frankly at the top of one poem, a generalization, "Happiness Makes Up in Height for What It Lacks in Length." That's *very* sweeping, and could be very deadly to some kind of people. They ought to say, "That's too simple." You see, they seem to have been taught that. I have heard old and young of the educated kind say, "Well, that's too simple."

Take Darwin's generalization about the survival of the fittest and the whole thing turning on that. We know that, you know, you can kick holes in that. There are troubles with it and

135

all that. But it's one of the wonderful generalizations. And it ought to make a difference in my life, now that I know I'm descended from monkeys.

I came from San Francisco — brought up near the Chinese, if not among 'em (another generalization) — and I'm naturally an ancestor worshipper. And since I found out I'm descended from monkeys, I think every morning, "What shall I do today to be worthy of my ancestry?" And do you know what I've decided? Another generalization: pick fleas off people. [. . .]

Now, let me tell you what I'm going to say to some Russians. This is another generalization. I'm going to say that our democracy is a traditional food. We've lived on it for two thousand years, like our bill of fare — with some food fads and all that mixed in, you know; but general food, wheat and so on. Our democracy is that. Theirs is an extract of democracy; the vitamins taken out of the food by Doctor Marx.

Any socialism, any communism is more or less strong vitamin extract of our democracy [. . .]. And when they offer me a spoonful of vitamins that are enough to last me a week, I just say, "I like a little roughage, too."

It's characteristic of our democracy that it's about two-thirds roughage — three-fourths roughage; I don't care how much. That's what it's all about. That's why we have trouble within ourselves. And we trust each other to have trouble with each other. The deadliness of the other is its purity. [. . .]

What do you say to this one, a historical one? (The poems are all that, all generalizations. But let me make another one.) The issue in the world for the last three hundred or four hundred years, the great issue — (There's just been one, one great issue. Probably you've already made it, what I'm going to say.) — the great issue has been to see what country would dominate with its character what Columbus discovered.

And the British did it. They put the French out. They put the Dutch out. They put the Spanish out. Elizabeth began it, and that's what it's been about. [. . .]

Oh, I could go on indefinitely about it. I live on 'em. And they're in the poems. In this one —— (I forgot that I'd said it, almost, till I talk to you now.) Once in one called "Build Soil," I said this very thing about socialism: that it belongs in every form of government. There's socialism monarchical; there's democratic socialism. It's just like vitamins in the food, scattered through the different foods. Take it all out pure and it's the hell. That's all; it ends in fearful cruelty. All purities do. You've got to say that.

Well, now for something else. For instance, here's one to begin with. I don't want you to watch too carefully after this, but you can notice in this first one what a generalization it is. It's about the Revolutionary War, and 'twas used as a frontispiece in an anthology of American poetry right in England. And I went over there and recited it around various places.

It's based on the generalization that the great conflicts of the world and the great tragedies are conflict of good and good, not good and bad — not necessarily good and bad. Ours was a conflict of good and good. The British colonial system was a good thing, but we got going ourselves. It's in the first line, the generalization: "The land was ours before we were the land's." [. . .]

[Mr. Frost said his poem "The Gift Outright."]

I said it in England, made the generalization, that their colonies were going the same way. And they laughed and said: "Well, yes, they're ripening off. You fell off green." That was a nice generalization.

This is all good-natured. What you want to be is as inclusive and comprehensive in everything you think and say, to

137

gather as much as you can. Maybe a little gets left out, spilled off. But don't let that bother you too much. You don't want to stick at trifles, do you? There's another generalization.

There are two generalizations. One, you mustn't be unscrupulous, must you? But you don't want to stick at trifles. Not the same thing; you don't want to stick at trifles, but you don't want to be unscrupulous. That's a kind of conflict in reason. Never mind.

But, now, take some of the simple poems and forget all this. But every one of 'em is dangerous; some of 'em very subversive. Generalizations; I ought to be caught at 'em. I'm just giving the enemy a chance. [. . .]

You know the most inclusive word in the world, the greatest generalization of all? One word, three letters: "God," of course.

Some of 'em don't want that anymore. My friend Julian Huxley says there is no God. There isn't any; it's a generalizing idea, very comprehensive. He thinks there's nothing but "it," the universe.

That's a form of pantheism. The old word for that, the old generalization for that, is "pantheism" — "it," the itness of the "it." And he thinks "it" has a kind of a stomachache, and that's us. It's all right, these are generalizations.

But the "God" is an interesting one. And you don't need that word. You know, the most wonderful word to me, short of that, is "purpose" — to generalize again. That's a big one: purpose, design, intention. And that applies to everything that's written and thought. Is there purpose in it?

You know what's the matter with a good many of the doctor's theses that get published, even, and never read? The trouble with them is they don't have enough design in 'em so you can get anything to hold of — purpose.

And some people don't know what the universe is doing.

Julian Huxley, I think, thinks it rolled purposeless until it accidentally produced us and that purpose began with us.

Well, my idea there would be, that's a joke. I'd say, "It must have rolled with the purpose of producing us." See? So, there's purpose in it, anyway. And if there is, that's all I ask. That's what I mean — as near as I need to get to the word "God."

—at the University of Miami,
February 26, 1960:

IN EVERYTHING there is an institution waiting for you — in love, in learning. In love it's marriage. In learning it's colleges and things like that. [. . .]

I don't know whether love is better outside of the institution or in the institution. I don't know whether religion is better in the institution or outside of the institution. ("Stay-at-home Baptists," you know, they used to call those that didn't go to church.)

And it occurred to me that I'd never brought it home to myself what was outside of the institution that I call "poetry." Well, it must be the spirit of poetry, mustn't it? I'm talking about the spirit in each of those things. [. . .]

Now, I have to answer for the poetry. The spirit of poetry is in all this mass of prose that's written. The institution at its core is poetry. All through the ages that's been the institution. [. . .]

I've got to be the same about the institution poetry as I am about the institution marriage and the institution church and the institution college. And the institution poetry is rhyme and metre. And the spirit of it all, I hope is as much in the institution as it is outside the institution in all this damn prose.

"In on the Ground Floor"

Mr. Frost's talk and reading at Amherst College on April 14, 1961, came in the wake of a trip he had made abroad during March, one that had had as a principal commitment his being in Israel for several days as Samuel Paley Foundation Lecturer at the Hebrew University of Jerusalem. The Amherst occasion was within a setting—to which he makes allusion at the outset—of the college's having earlier in that same academic year installed a new president, Calvin H. Plimpton, who had but recently returned from a period of service as a member of the medical faculty at the American University of Beirut and as the chief of staff of its hospital.

I DON'T USUALLY take a subject to talk on, but suppose I say something under the head of "The Ground Floor" — "In on the Ground Floor." You think perhaps I'm going to speak of the new administration, but I'm not. But there is a certain newness about that, you see, and a freshness around it. That's what we wait for.

But I've just been in — as he's been — in a very old part of the world. And the noticeable thing of the old part where I've been is that everybody has the feeling of being in on the ground floor, in a new enterprise. They haven't had a country, the new country of Israel, very long. And I was aware everywhere that the young and old were keyed up with the enterprise, also the insecurity.

I go around sympathizing with little nations and multiplying little nations all I can. That's part of my business, to multiply nations, you know. But I've said I've been anxious for the little nations — as I had been for Finland, say — that could be wiped out at the caprice of some bigger thing at any moment.

The oil interests might wipe Israel out any day, and they know it. And so the insecurity is in it, too, with the newness, the freshness. And it's very stirring to me.

As I said to one notable person — (I said this to Rabbi Glueck, who was on the platform with me only a little while ago, praying. He prayed; quite a friend of mine.) — but I told him about this anxiety of mine for the little country. "Oh," he said, "we're so aware of it that we just forget it and go ahead loving and selling." Business of love and commerce.

And he said: "We never had any security, except under Solomon, anyway. And we had no business there, in the first place. We took the country away from the Canaanites." You see, very, very broad-minded he was about it.

But now I was thinking — (I'm going to tell you just one little anecdote before I start reading.) — I was thinking how long that spirit probably lasted in America.

Some prominent Jew over there said to a girl that was coming home to America, a Jewess, she said, "What do you go home to that empty life for in America?" (Did you see that in the paper?)

She said, "I don't think it's empty." And she said: "Stay here, why don't you? You could have lipstick here." And the girl said, "I don't use it." That was a nice one.

"Empty life," you know! The woman speaking — (We won't name names.) — the woman speaking was from Brooklyn. She's a heroic woman, great lady. But that was her attitude to America, that 'twas an empty life.

Just the routine of things can get you to feeling that way. But probably fifty years, you know —— It didn't take that long for some sort of disillusionment to happen in Ireland, before people began to be disillusioned about what they'd got.

What is your state? What is our state? How do we feel when

this is called an "empty life"? How did I feel when I read that in the paper? How do you feel when I say it, amused or mad — angry-mad? Resentful, I do; just sort of resentful. It doesn't stay with me too long. It's too small. But it's a kind of test. [. . .]

I'm going where I have to say something about another poet in a night or two. I've got to say something about a poet named Tagore. I don't know whether you ever read him. Everybody read him thirty years ago. And I knew him, a great Indian poet.

This is the hundredth anniversary of his death. No, of his birth, I mean. I'm going to have to say something about him, and I don't know what to make of him.

Do you know what they're doing — what they're all doing? They're trying to make him out as a link between the East and West and everything like that, a unifier of the world. But I knew him, personally, and he had more spirit of making a nation than I have. And I have plenty.

As I said, I'm all for the multiplication of nations. He was full of it, about India. And he had a lot to do with making India what it is today, a nation on its own.

It's Mr. Nehru and some of his old friends that are in this big affair. I think they're forgetting how nationalist he is. They're forgetting already their dedication to the new country. They're getting to be "One Worlders" or something like that. I'm afraid they are. I've got to see about that, anyway.

But here's a kind of little poem I wrote about it. This is called "The Courage to Be New." The greatest courage of all, the courage to be new; the most dangerous courage, too. It's a terrible danger — so original that you're afraid of yourselves, afraid of what you might do to the world.

And I'm all for you. Come tell me about it, will you, if you've got anything like that up your sleeve. I'll join you in the conspiracy, originality.

A certain restlessness

Mr. Frost's presence at the University of Massachusetts in Amherst on October 25, 1961, took place within a short time after the opening of the university's fall semester and as colleges across the country were beginning new academic years. His was the institution's first Alumni Memorial Lecture of 1961–62, and provision was made for its being broadcast nationally over the Educational Radio Network and for its delayed transmission, also, by the World-Wide Broadcasting Corporation.

"THESE ARE the days when the birds come back. . . ." Do you know who's talking now? It's not me.—

> These are the days when the birds come back,
> A very few, a bird or two,
> To take a backward look.[42]

And these days are described in the same poem as "A blue and gold mistake." Not my poetry.

These are the days when the kids come back, not "a very few," a *slew* — (You know what "slew" means? That's old slang, isn't it? That's gone out of date.) — to take a *forward* look; come back to college.

And I always think they may be like me. They come back to show what they can do — dying to show what they can do in football — or dying to tell something they've thought of all summer or during the summer — something that's happened to 'em or something that's occurred 'em. [. . .]

Now, I always come back with something — however unrelated to the situation. I come back with something just from sheer desire to tell it.

I'd like to connect it with you this way. I think so many of you are like people that are just going somewhere socially or spatially, and you don't think its worth thinking about where you are. You know, we're just about to go into space, or we're just about to become communists or socialists or something, and what's the use of paying any attention to this.

That don't mean about school, but just about life in general. There's a certain restlessness, of somebody that's all dressed up to go somewhere and nowhere to go.

Two things I thought of this summer, among many others, that I'm dying to tell somebody — anybody I can catch — have to do with that.

You want to know the most conservative thing in the world? (You see, you hear about conservatism and radicalism.) Do you want to know the most radical thing in the world? I'll tell you. I've just thought of 'em.

The most conservative thing in the world is that in birth like produces like. Human beings don't have animals for children; they have human beings. That's the most conservative thing of all, that that goes on. Then, the most radical thing in the world is a certain dissatisfaction with that fact.

And I'm going to tell you more about that. I'm an "evolutionary man," as Mr. Julian Huxley calls him. I am *The — The —* evolutionary man. (You see, with a capital "*The.*") I know all about it — just as much as he knows. He's in the business, and I'm just an amateur.

But put this this way. He would be sure that that dissatisfaction meant that we were going to be supermen right away. I'm very uncertain about that.

The dissatisfaction is a certain restlessness, in the human

being, that has brought us to where we are. It's in nature — that restless in nature — as if some sort of force was chafing at the bit, you know, to get on. And it's moving in us. [. . .]

We should so conduct ourselves as evolutionary men, you'd think, that it will be a shorter distance from us to superman than it was from monkeys to us. Think that over.

But I warn you — (This is the way I'm going to close this thought.) — I warn you that this restlessness in us may be a dead-end thing. It may have brought us to here and will never carry us any further.

I suspect it's a dead-end thing. We're not going any further, except in civilization. We aren't going to have any more legs than we've got or any more heads than we've got — or tails, either. 'Tisn't going to be different. Nobody knows, you know; but I'm warning you.

They seem not to have thought of that, my contemporaries, that this restlessness that I have such a respect for — that makes us feel all the time a dissatisfaction (What they like to call a "divine dissatisfaction" — something divine in it; it may be divine.) — it brought us to where we are, but it's a dead-end. It's not going to carry us any further.

On the evolutionary tree — the tree of life — it's some other branch may go somewhere. We're not going any further — except in civilization. That's another thing; that's not in evolution at all — civilization.

All right, that's that. Then, one thing more I thought of that I want to tell you.

I keep coming onto the feeling that — (This same "divine dissatisfaction"; if you want to call it.) — that this isn't much of a country. Very widespread, that sort of criticism that's going on in all our literature and in all the talk.

And I thought of this summer, that maybe we don't know

how good we are. But I tell you who does know how good we are, the Russians. They look in our direction every time they speak, just as you do in company with the most important person present. That's the other one.

Now, I started with Emily Dickinson about this. (That was down the street, she used to live; downstreet here.) This restlessness, it's wrought there. And it has to do with our originality in our civilization and on the football field and everywhere.

You know, I'm always sorry that the new ideas of football aren't the boys' so much as the coaches'. I think that's rather sad. I like to think the boys are original. And I like to think that the originality is everywhere.

The thing I crave the most is to feel that all over the educational world everybody has got something on his mind he's crazy to tell me if he gets a chance, just the same as I'm crazy to tell you.

That's my nature, and I expect other people to be like. And I want to respect their variance — their departure, their originality. I want to hear from them.

— at Trinity College, October 11, 1962:

A PROFESSOR of considerable standing said to me the other day — (I've been with him a good many times.) — he said, "I never saw a head so full of bad poetry as yours."

I said to him: "Charlie, that's fatal. If it's in my head it means it's a good poem. If I know it, it's a good poem. That's the way I know it's good, because it's memorable. That's what poetry was written for in the first place, to be memorable, so you couldn't get it out of your head."

About thinking and
of perishing to shine

Mr. Frost's 1962 appearance at Agnes Scott, for the talk and reading of January twenty-fifth from which this excerpt has been drawn, was heralded in both the student and local-area press as being his twentieth visit (dating from 1935), to the Decatur, Georgia, women's college.

I HAVE OFTEN thought that I like a lot of chances to set myself right with people, and yet not try to be too definite and defining — just sort of feel my way with them.

I'm an *invidious* — insidious — no, let's say that I'm an *insidious* nationalist, if you know what that is. You'd know that without my saying it. It's all scattered through my poems, what a terrible American I am — *terrible*. You get used to it. If you see enough of it, you don't mind it, anyway. You can stand it, no matter what your politics are. [. . .]

Now, I was going to say a few words about a given subject. I've told people once or twice that I once gave a lecture on how you can tell when you're thinking. I go around and tell about the time I gave that lecture. I haven't repeated it. They're not written down, you know.

They ask me don't I want to give it tonight? I say: "That's a very expensive lecture. I keep that for big money." It's a secret, I tell 'em, how you can tell when you're thinking. But there's a little you can say about it [. . .].

I mean something beyond just opinionating. That's like voting, you know. I vote against women's voting, say. "That's your

147

opinion," we'll say. (You girls don't believe in voting, I suppose.) "That's just your opinion. Haven't you got any more to say about it than that? And if you haven't got any more to say about it, don't tell me."

That's not thinking. That's opinionating. Agreeing with me isn't thinking. That's not what I mean.

I tell you, all thinking comes down to this word "sharp" — that we use in slang almost: "He's very sharp. He's very sharp tonight." That means he missed no chances to be reminded, by what was going on, of something interesting related to it. His mind is easily reminded — well-reminded; he's right up, fresh. That's the best of all things. [. . .]

The readiness with which you're reminded by what's going on, reminded of what's distant in time — books, life, and so on — aptly reminded. The word "reminding" is all there is to thinking. And every good thought that counts as a thought is a feat of association like that.

Just say that, for me. That's the heart of it all, a feat of association. You make a good, apt association, to the pleasure of everybody.

Now, we use the word "happy" thought, in the wrong way. It's corrupted. It's sunk down. What it originally meant was just that: that happy association — not a cheerful association, not something that makes you happy; something that charms you because it's fresh and original.

The word "original" will do for it. (I don't like the word too much.) I don't know; not necessarily greatly original, but it's a fresh, fresh reminding. [. . .]

I have to speak with some feeling of sorrow. Robinson Jeffers has just died, my distant friend. I never knew him very well. He kept himself in his tower in California, and I never go to towers. But I admired him. I admired his pessimism. And just for

148

that, that it was a fresh, original pessimism—very dark, bitter.

And what a fine figure this is for throwing life away, you know. It's not my figure. But it's his—and a good one and a bad one; the worse it is the better. He says, "Give your heart to the hawks." It's the title of the poem.

That's all you need. That's all there is to life: "Give your heart to the hawks." He died in that spirit. Touching.

I never tried to deal with that. I just took it as a good black spot in my thoughts. But he said something that I was confronted with. (That doesn't confront me. I know all that sentiment in other writers. It's an ancient one: "Give your heart to the hawks." It's a pretty way to put it.) But he says "shine, perishing republic" to us—"shine, perishing republic."[43] And I used that, happened to use it, in my new book that was gone to press before I knew all about his death. Just one line: "shine, perishing republic."

What are you going to do with that? Either let it alone or include it in my book. And the way I include it is that everything that shines, shines by perishing—candles, the sun, and *me*.

And then I don't know what he does with it. That's what I do with it. I think he's darker than that. Mine is everything shines by perishing, everything. And you've got to remember that. It's a great, great thought. But mine includes his.

And how long will the United States shine before it perishes? (I always say—you know, talking about money—I tell 'em I always charge more for prophecy than I do for history.) I don't know how long we're going to last. The song says, "It shall wave a thousand years."[44]

That's a good long time. We've only spent two hundred of it. Thousand is—if you look in history—it's a good long time. It's longer than most have done it. The great days of a nation are seldom anything like that. You've got to think of that.

And what shall we do while we are spending, while we're burning through our lives? That you ask yourself as you look around today. We're squandering our light, almost, to the world. It's wonderful we are; wonderful shining thing we are. But you wonder about the economy of it. We have to ask the economists.

I'm not trying to frighten you. I'm not scared if you're not. But a thousand years evolves, you know. We've got lots of time to turn around in that time.

But don't think we're forever. We can't be. Nothing is forever. Everything shines to perish, perishes to shine. And so that takes you out of all the little quibbling thoughts of the day.

Here we are, the richest nation in the world — the richest nation the world has ever seen, with the widest diffusion of wealth that the world has ever seen — and shining as such, so that everybody looks in this direction. And if we're troubled by our responsibility of shining to perish, we're a small lot, petty-minded. Big, let's make it big and shine.

And to measure it all the time, you know. We don't need to just burn like a prairie fire. That was Tom Paine's idea of democracy. It was going to be a prairie fire that swept the world. This isn't like that. This is a great steady flame — like Sirius, like the star Sirius, and like the sun — as we shine.

Nobody knows in the universe anything that isn't spending. One of the strange things, the confidences, that the scientists get up for themselves is that something must be coming in. They haven't any evidence of it anywhere, not a glimmer of it. Everything is spending, spending — grand, grand spending.

We're not talking about terms, what the terms are. They're vast terms, little terms, and all that.

Well, the point is, though, that's just my handling of something I encounter. I see that "shine, perishing republic," and I know there's a certain note of pessimism in his poem. Without reading further, I know just how he'll take it. But I know another way to take it: everything shines; perishes to shine.

That's just what I mean by thinking. That's all there is to thinking: feat of association. And it's better never to take anything head on, contradict it. If you can, sort of outwit it — go it one better, by some liveness in your own mind, live mind. And remind, remind. [. . .]

I've had to say lately, to myself, what I'm around for. I'm around for my poems, chiefly. And I'm not around preaching. And I'm not around teaching. I just found this out: I'm around looking for kindred spirits, for their comfort and mine. And I do it on a percentage basis.

But that's what is. I'm wandering around — like butterflies in the air, you know — looking for kindred spirits. That's all, not preaching or teaching.

You don't have to agree with anything I say. You don't have to get mad at me, 'cause I don't get mad at you. And I'm not out for any particular cause. I belong to causes, but I'm very, very, very happy in my relation to 'em. [. . .]

I've shown you — sort of what I call in a loose, scattered way; not loose, but a scattered way — about what I mean by thinking — not arguing, not pressing; no, presenting — that I've shown myself as a person sharply reminded of this, that, and the other thing in the universe, when I'm feeling right. (Sometimes when I'm not really feeling right, I just wonder where it's gone.) That's all there is to it, the condition that makes you kind of sharp about being reminded. You sometimes blame yourself when you should have been reminded by something, and somebody else is better, does it for you.

In history — just one word more — there was a great historian named Gibbon. And I remember reading very young, in a little preface to the history of Rome, *The Decline and Fall* — a little preface about him, years ago — that as he was dying he was still at — they said — still at his old historical parallels. He was always being reminded of one thing by another. He died with those parallels and surprising people with his parallels; connections, associations, you see.

That had a lot to do with my life — just thinking and beginning to see that — that when you're good, mentally good, your parallels are good, your life.

—at Amherst College, April 21, 1958:

This subject is always the subject up in reading poetry:

There are three meanings, you might say. There's the first meaning, the surface meaning; and the second, intimation that the poet is more or less aware of. (In painting it's the same, you know; in any art. There's the ulterior, always the ulterior.)

And, then, there seems to be another something that is the question, "What's the matter with the author; what's eating him?" And, you see, that always bothers me a good deal. I'm willing to have 'em going on that way and glad to have 'em interested in me, of course. [. . .]

My tendency is to simplify the ulterior. There is always something that's around the edges of it. And you can always make a pretty turn of it. I don't mind what they do to it, as long as they don't debase it. If they go me one better in it — make something amusing out of it, make something prettier than I made — that's all right. But to debase it, it bothers me.

A gentler interest in the fine things

Robert Frost began his presentation at the University of Michigan on April 2, 1962, with references to his own intervals there at Ann Arbor — first, as Poet in Residence and, then, as Fellow in Creative Arts — during the early 1920s, making special mention in doing so of Marion LeRoy Burton, who, following presidencies at both Smith College and the University of Minnesota, had headed the University of Michigan from 1920 until his death in 1925, and of Raymond Mollyneaux Hughes, president of Ohio's Miami University from 1913 to 1927 and subsequently of Iowa State College.

JUST BEFORE I start reading, I want to say to you I wonder what's come over us — the country, you know — that everything is so for me and younger poets and all. There's so much excitement about us. It's got so that we can hardly keep out of national politics, and no designs at all.

But it began, you might say, right in the colleges and universities. It began with the president of this university, for one, about forty-odd years ago, Mr. Burton, my friend.

I had seen him once when he was at Smith College, in my neighborhood, in New England. And then he asked me out — (I don't know whether he was in my audience or not.) — he asked me out to speak at Minnesota. And then he asked me here to live, and I saw a great deal of him.

His idea was one of the initial ideas in this all. I know four or five or six poets now that are among the privileged few in the academic world. They haven't anything to do but "rake the leaves where the gentle zephyrs blowed 'em," as somebody said. They have very pleasant lives. [. . .]

In this with Mr. Burton was President Hughes of Oxford, Ohio. And their idea was to have one poet a year or one artist a year, one painter or one musician. And that was all.

And that was a mistake. It didn't work. They didn't get 'em. There weren't enough to get one a year and keep it up for forty years. Something was lacking.

And it came into this other thing, with a sort of a privileged connection, with the universities as patrons — as if the universities must take the place of the aristocracy in Europe in patronizing the arts. That came into their heads. And I saw all that happening.

After they tried the first way one year, then the president said to me: "You've done nothing but go out to dinner, the whole year. I'm going to give you a year in hiding here." So, I came another year to hide. I didn't hide very successfully.

Then, that was over, and they went looking for other kinds of people. And they had no luck about it.

One mistake was in trying to get a dramatist. And a dramatist is either so good that he makes so much money he won't come to things like this, or he isn't very interesting. It was a nice case of dramatists — gentlemen and all that. But it wasn't what they meant by stirring up any excitement.

And then Mr. Burton himself — very enterprising man — he lit out for England and brought home the Poet Laureate of England, for a year. He came for part of a year. I was brought out here to welcome him and tell him not to be afraid of the rough western boys. [. . .]

And Mr. Meiklejohn, a famous college president, was another of my benefactors in this similar way. I was back and forward between here and Amherst College, between the two places.

Now it's gone on. I really think that the educator world sort of melted toward us contemporaries. They used to be very proud of not reading anybody later than the eighteenth century. But they began to melt, in this way.

And at last we've got a department — not a department — an office of the fine arts in the White House, with two friends of mine in charge of it; and presiding over them, the President and his wife.

Isn't it pretty? And I hope it will stay right in the White House — (I've just been down there with it all.) — and I hope it will stay in the White House and won't go out into a big building, all departmental. But I don't know that it can. The Congress is getting excited, too, and all that.

And, you know, a country like this — so rich, so great in riches and the diffusion of riches; the greatest the world has ever seen — has reached a point, I think, where it can afford to be considerate of nice things.

And considerateness in affairs, it looks sometimes a little weak and a little timid or something. We're so considerate of other nations' feelings, we hesitate to go at it before we're sure there's any issue. We're looking for the issue all the time.

And that's considerateness. That's one of our great virtues. But it's a dangerous one, you know. But it's the virtue that we can afford now. I watch it with a great deal of interest.

Just that word "considerateness" — and the word "weak"; the "weak" is a great word. I'm willing to take favors from people who give them out of a conscientious concern for me, but I like people better who have a weakness for me and the arts. [. . .]

There's a new sort of thing in Washington. I used to think Washington was the coldest city in the world for me to read in. I read there sometimes, but it was cold to me. And so the buildings looked cold. And now they all look warm.

That's been happening in two administrations. It's not just

this one. Mr. Eisenhower was in this, too, very much — though he's not a reading man. But neither was George Washington.

You probably don't know it, but George Washington tried to write a poem once. It's in existence still, partly written. 'Twas to a girl, and he never got through with it quite. I think they have it in the archives. I've seen it somewhere. But that wasn't his line. He was a great general. [. . .]

All this that I'm talking about, this melting that I feel in the country and in the educational world — (I live with these universities and colleges; that's where my life is.) — I take it that it's something that's come over us in our affluence, belongs to the affluence of a great nation coming into an age of affluence and caring for fine things — a gentler interest in the fine things and a passing out of the boorish — (The "boorish" we'll call it; just the crude and rude and the go-after-everything.) — just something easing off.

—at Yale University, May 19, 1961:

SOMEBODY asked me in Israel the other day if I believed in education. I said, "Yes, yes, yes." See, just like that. And they said, "Why do you believe in it?" I said — (I was cornered.) — I said, "It lifts trouble and sorrow to a higher plane of regard." I don't say it gets over it, makes any difference in it; it lifts it to a higher plane of regard, as in *King Lear.*

They quoted that in the paper, but they left off the plane "of regard"; they lifted it "to a higher plane." That meant it made a bed of sorrow or something. I didn't mean that, I meant it lifted it to a higher plane of regard.

156

Let's say bravely . . . that poetry counts

On October 13, 1962, Mr. Frost was a participant in Mount Holyoke College's observance of the one hundred and twenty-fifth anniversary of its existence as an institution devoted to the education of women. And in the course of his remarks he pointed out that it was for him personally a time of celebration, too, this centering upon his having earlier in the year — on the occasion of his eighty-eighth birthday — published a new book of his poetry, entitled *In the Clearing*. Also, he made reference to his visit to the Soviet Union, for the U. S. Department of State, which had taken place little more than a month earlier.

I'M GOING TO write a book on college presidents someday. I've known quite a lot of 'em. And I might tell you right now, the book's going to turn on one sentence, with a semicolon in it, I guess: "The college presidents are to be divided into two kinds;" — (from my point of view and yours, too) — "those that have a conscientious concern for our things and those who have a weakness for them." Our things, you know; can't let 'em alone.

There's quite a story to tell about it, make a little book that I threatened a long time to write. I started it on an occasion like this, once years ago — thought of it then, about the president I was with. He was resigning; one of the lovely ones who had a strong weakness for our things.

You see, I say "our things," plural. I don't say "my thing" — "our things." And that brings me to the question of what I mean by "our things" and whose are they? I get asked about that a good many times as I kick around. I've been asked it twice the last two visits I've made.

157

I sit round sometimes with the boys afterward and the girls, and I get asked if poetry matters much in the world — (I got asked that in another country, even.) — and who does it matter to, if it matters to anybody?

And then they ask, "Does it matter more to women than to men?" Then, I always tell 'em that if I catch a man reading my book — red-handed, you know; guilty — catch him reading my book, he usually looks up and says, "My wife's a great fan of yours." Puts it off on the ladies.

Then, pressed further about that: "What you writing poetry for?" Well, like any other thing. Somebody asks me, in a religious way if it was a sort of "offering." Yes, on the altar of something. (That makes you think, "Here's a good Congregationalist; doesn't mind some Old Testament in his life.")

One of the greatest prayers in the world is the one — (I think maybe it's repeated. I don't know how many times. But it always stays in my mind as one of the big, big, big things in my life.) — the prayer, "May my sacrifice be acceptable in Thy sight."[45]

That's your life if you die on the battlefield. That's your poem. That's your everything. It means to sacrifice — means the whole of you, you know, into it — and still the fear of God. You see, that's the fear of God — that it's still a question: Is it acceptable in His sight?

What does that mean in our English language? Does what I do amount to anything? Does it count? And we don't know. That's where you launch off into your religion, with that prayer: May it count; may what I do count.

In Russia, I said the other day that I suppose the men of action in the world accorded poetry something, though they get far from it most of the time. But they accord a place.

And it's similar to the place they accord women. They grant that women, in some sense of the word, "run" the world. And in that same sort of sense, they might grant that poetry does. They might smile at this claim of a poem you probably know that says:

> We, in the ages lying
>> In the buried past of the earth,
> Built Nineveh with our sighing,
>> And Babel itself with our mirth:
> And o'erthrew them with prophesying
>> To the new of the old world's worth;
> For each age is a dream that is dying . . .

A dream, you see.—

Or one that is coming to birth.[23]

That's sort of the claim of it, its own claim. I leave that to you, and I leave that to the world. But I think the men might grant that, in the way they grant that women have really run the world—in the same way—and maybe that poetry might be called the "link place" between men and women, about all that, with the women having the strong hold on it at the one end. But those are just thoughts about it.

The boys are a great crowd to read to, talk to. And does poetry with me get more political with them? I sometimes get sick of the puny poetry that thinks money's a bad thing and that men are a bad thing and that power is a bad thing.

I've been joking about liberals, so that I've got to write a book about them pretty soon, to satisfy people.

For instance, I say that a liberal is one who would rather fuss with a Gordian Knot than cut it. And then I could say, more seriously, that a liberal has his doubts about anything that's arbitrary. He doesn't realize that the height of it all is the arbitrary—even where we vote about every day of our lives; we vote, vote, vote, vote.

I've been with a head of a steel company—just brought me up here today—one of the steel companies. He's chairman of

159

the board now. He's retired from the presidency and all that. But he's a man who's lived somewhat an arbitrary life. You ask him if his board ever tells him what to do or vote what to do. No, they just accept it when he tells them that he's done it. He's an arbitrary man.

The head of my publishing house confessed that. I search 'em; how much is voted — voted approval? (They say that a manly head of a big company said, "All those in favor say 'aye'; the rest of you resign." And that's illiberal, you know.)

With me, this isn't anything new at all. It runs all through my poems, if you notice them — for those that care about that sort of side of things, the political and all. The very life of the country, it depends something on that.

It says, "It shall wave" — our flag — it says, "It shall wave a thousand years."[44] So, it's liberal and progressive to give the country away as fast as you can, before the thousand years are up. You see, spend it; see, give it all. Give it to the poor. Give it to the —— Well, what shall I call 'em?

Sometimes I say about *them* that if I ran it — (I don't run it, of course.) — if I ran the country, I wouldn't run it to disembarrass the good-for-nothing, so as to make them think when they go on relief it's an honorary degree. You see, there's my leaning — though I'm a Democrat. (One thing you can say about the Democratic party is that there's more kinds of Democrats to be than there are kinds of Republicans; it's looser.)

And to finish up about all this and get to the poems; I think my poems belong to politics, religion, and history and all. And I hate to have that forgotten for a minute. And if I get into affairs of the world and feel pleased to be in 'em, it's because I want my poetry to be like that.

I want it to count with men as much as with women. With women in their way; and men, probably it's through women to men that I get there, a good deal, you know — a good deal.

160

I have a great experience of it. I'm very, very, very experienced and know all about it. I can tell a good deal by who puts the finger on the right word somewhere in the poetry — who says just one word in some one place.

I can't tell by questionnaire. I've never found out anything by questionnaire. The liberals send around questionnaires. I never got out questionnaires, even when I was teaching. [. . .]

I give somebody "A" for life if he says the right thing at the right moment about the right thing. And I give 'em "D" for life if they say just one wrong thing that shows they just don't know what it's all about. That's all.

And it goes clear into your religion, your Bible. The height of religion is that prayer I said to you. That's the fear of God that you hear liberals say you must get over. No fears at all; don't have any fears anymore, children.

But you'd better be afraid of God, in that sense: You don't know whether you count with Him. And a pagan would say, "It's on the lap of the gods." It means practically the same thing. Your fate is "on the lap of the gods" — and your acceptance, you know; what you write.

You've got to remember that, when I read you poems and things, that I read them in that fear of God. I'm not afraid of you. [. . .]

Well, this is a celebration, sort of, of yours and one for me, too. I've got a new book, you know. I leaf over it myself, and if somebody mentions something in it — especially some boy or girl — that's my favorite poem for the time being. I feel, "Oh, well, I'll have another look at that; that's a very good poem, isn't it?"

But beyond all that is what I speak of, the fear of God.— Does it count? And how does it count?

Just one word more: how it counts. It counts, if it counts, somewhat politically.

Again, to make a rather amusing distinction, there's two

things; there's grievance and grief. A grievance is something that something can be done about, political sort of a thing. That's politics, statescraft, everything — grievances to correct and handle. And grief is in the lines that I've said to some a number of times lately. Out of the fifteenth century, I guess it is. It says:

> I know my life's a pain and but a span;
> I know my sense is mock'd in everything;
> And, to conclude, I know myself a Man —
> Which is a proud and yet a wretched thing.[4]

That's a grief. That's the grief of it that stays there. And poetry has a happy-sad way of talking about that a lot of the time. There's a song — (A college song, I think it is.) — that struck me years ago. I don't know it very well. But it had for a refrain in it, about drink, that it would "make you happy, make you sad." Happy-sad; that's the poetry of it. That's the grief of it: the brevity of our life, the span, and our not knowing what's still bothering us. And the poetry deals with that. But also it comes into reforms.

I think when I'm asked if it counts very much, if it does much — (Does it go in for reforms? Is it in favor of doing this or that?) — it's a lower class of poetry that gets down to politics. And when I get down to politics, I know I'm sort of a little shallower. It's deeper when it's with the happy-sad. [. . .]

Well, leave that; leave it a little happy-sad — sometimes with tears. Isn't this odd, that in that poem —

> We, in the ages lying
>   In the buried past of the earth,
> Built Nineveh with our sighing,
>   And Babel itself with our mirth. . . .[23]

there are the two things again? But why he gave them to Nineveh and Babylon, I've always wondered. Was Nineveh a sad place? Were they a sophisticated sad city, with that kind of beautiful melancholy touch? Was their beauty that kind? And was the other a sort of riotous mirth, you know, coarser lower-class?

In poetry, they really blend. But it's a pretty thing, that pairing again in Babel and Nineveh — mirth and sadness — isn't it? They're there. And the strangest blend of all, the wonderfulest thing of all, is the happy-sad blend of just that sort of low-class song about drink:

> Sadly thinking,
> With . . .

Let's see.—

> With spirits sinking . . .

Let's see if I can say that poem.—

> Sadly thinking,
> With spirits sinking,
> Would more than drinking
> My cares compose —
> A cure for sorrow
> From sighs I'd borrow;
> And hope tomorrow
> Would end my woes.
> But since in wailing
> There's naught availing,
> And Death, unfailing,
> Will strike the blow;
> Then, for this reason,
> And for a season,
> Let us be merry
> Before we go! . . .[46]

That's an Irish one, in this same play with all that. Well, I'm tempted to linger about it all. I've seen so much about it lately, the pros and cons of it all.

Let's say bravely, we girls, that poetry counts. Not necessarily mine, but it counts.

—at New York University,
March 23, 1956:

NEARLY EVERYTHING I get into is unpremeditated. That's my happy life, fortunate life.

I'm just academic enough, you know, to be a teacher. And I'm just farmer enough to be a farmer. And I'm just poet enough, I guess, to be called a poet.

I never got called that till I was forty. And I was embarrassed when I was first called it, though I'd been writing for twenty years. But all of it's been kind of haphazard and accidental.

Somebody asked me once, when I began to make up my mind that I'd write poetry. I said I never dared to let anybody know I'd made up my mind, if I had. It was more or less my own private affair; and I went ahead and wrote little poems. I wrote 'em because I couldn't let 'em alone, because I fell into rhyme and metre at the age of fifteen, in a high school where there was no English taught. [. . .]

I had no courses in English. All I had was Latin and Greek and mathematics and a little tiny bit of history. But the whole course of high school and college to me was just Latin and Greek and mathematics; no English at all.

I'll tell you a little about my walks

During the autumn of 1962, still actively "barding around," speaking and giving readings of his poems before both college and community audiences across the nation, Mr. Frost traveled to Michigan in order to receive on November thirteenth an honorary Doctor of Humane Letters degree from the University of Detroit. The "evening of poetry and informal talk," excerpted from here, which took place at the university on the following day, proved to be one of the last of the poet's platform appearances. Less than a month later he entered a Boston hospital, where he died on January 29, 1963, just eight weeks before his eighty-ninth birthday.

I COUNT CITIES mine, my trophies in my life, if I've talked in them, but more particularly if I've slept in 'em and walked in 'em alone. It begins with San Francisco, and it's just now got to Detroit. [. . .] I'll tell you a little about my walks in them when I read you some of my poems.

You know, poetry seems in the past to have been chiefly of the country. But it always sells itself in the city. And that goes way back.

There's a general antagonism that they're trying to work up nowadays between the country and the city, as if the city was an awful thing. There's been a book about it lately by a couple of professors.

It's an old story. It's like the antagonism between town and gown. That's almost died. But they're working up this again. It's a kind of a Thoreausian thing. Thoreau hated cities, I guess. People don't see why they all want to come to the city.

You see, the word "city" is in our word "police." It's in our word "policy." It's in our word "polite." It's the Greek word always.

And "polish"; I presume the word "polish," what you call "polish," is a city thing. The country thing is a little uncouth, and sometimes affects a certain uncouthness, to sell itself to the city. It's a strange, strange situation. I've never been caught in that thing.

My walks have been country walks, somewhat. But my first memory of a long walk is up California Street in San Francisco, all alone — when we lived up that way; when I was eight and ten years old, in those two years, when I came away.

And a good many of my poems mention the word "walk." I think of it now when I see "DON'T WALK" and "WALK" in the city. You see: "WALK" / "DON'T WALK."

I'm the only walker. I walked this afternoon for one hour and only met two people on foot. That's right; I counted 'em. I walked the whole hour.

And part of my walking that never brought me much into Detroit before was in Ann Arbor, three years. I walked it up and down and all around. And I might as well begin with a poem that sort of sprung from that. 'Twasn't that city; it's city in general. But I remember writing it there.

> [Mr. Frost said his poem
> "Acquainted with the Night."]

That light that I'm thinking of — that clock proclaiming "the time was neither wrong nor right" — was certainly in Ann Arbor. I remember the look of it.

Now, to go on — not to make too much of this antagonism between the country and the city — cities have been where people gathered to sell their vegetables and sell their poetry, ever since time began. There's no reason why there should be this kind of literature going on, right now, about the dreadfulness of these big cities.

I get the same thing about the big universities, they're so huge. And I say if we go in for bigness, let's go in; let's not apologize for it. These great cities give me confidence. They hold the continent down.

The strange thing is to talk against the suburbs as if they were a tangle of snakelike roads, choking the world or something. I saw that somewhere the other day. And, of course, all the going out into the country, into the suburbs, means a general kind of longing for a touch of the country, to go out there.

So many people I know worked in the big city and would live in the big city, but they have little children to think of, and they want them to have some ground to run around on. They're seeking the country for them.

One thing I tell you they're seeking, they're seeking a woodshed and some tools, so that you don't have to take 'em down into the basement of the schoolhouse and teach them how to pound with a hammer, drive a nail — have it going on naturally more, outside. It's a kind of a compromise thing, but a thing to praise, an adjustment. Wonderful!

You ride through miles of it. You hear talk as if everything was in decay. But everything looks *fine*, pretty suburbs.

I know people who go home an hour and a half from New York City, clear to Princeton. And my publisher, the president of my firm, goes home to New Canaan, an hour and a half each way; and says he reads on the way, so it's all right.

And that was for the children. You'll find that in both those cases — for the children, and give them a touch of country life; not much, but a little.

But the refinement — the "polish" — and the "polite" — "police" — (Polite police; that's a funny combination!) — all get their name from the word "city," "city," "city." So, I just wanted to say that.

Then, let's go on and talk about walking a little more. I've walked so many miles, and the word "walking" comes into so many of my poems — and the "town." [. . .]

But my string of cities, should I name 'em to you? This last one in the string is Detroit, where I walked an hour today and where I slept. San Francisco, first; and, then, Lawrence, Massachusetts; then, New York; then, Boston; then, Miami; and, then, London; and, most recently, where I walked alone — (I don't count it unless I've walked alone.) — Moscow.

That's my string so far. I could remember others perhaps, but those are the chief ones. And if you were just to my poems — if you want to be just to 'em at all — you'll know that I don't join in this antagonism between city and country. I'm a mixed creature, very mixed — confused, maybe, by it. That's what they say, you know. [. . .]

I said when I was getting my honorary degree yesterday that it was funny the way I had got to be "educated by degrees." I never went through college, you know; never went through it — just "educated by degrees." And I made a joke out of it once: "degree-dation" — degree-giving dation. You see, that's Latin: degreedation. That's the way I've got educated.

I said it just went to show how, if it was in you to get educated, you couldn't escape.

Editor's Note

. .

References

.

Index

Editor's Note — GRATEFUL ACKNOWLEDGMENT IS MADE to libraries and archives that have provided voice recordings of the Robert Frost presentations from which excerpts have been drawn and are featured within this volume — most particularly to the Amherst College Library for use of its extensive holding of such resources, gathered from various institutions and organizations throughout the United States and abroad, and spanning a period of more than two decades, as well as to the Dartmouth College Library for its provision of tapes representing the poet's participation in Dartmouth's Great Issues Course, 1947–1962, and other of his platform appearances at the College.

The principal units of the collection are arranged chronologically by date of delivery. Short supplementary segments have been placed where opportunity of space permitted, without consideration of time sequence or whether coverage therein relates to what immediately precedes or follows. Titles for the excerpts have been editorially supplied, unless specification to the contrary is given.

Within the texts, fragmentary and incomplete expression — typically consisting of tentative beginnings, abandoned in favor of another choice of words or a different manner of proceeding — has been omitted without indication of incidence. Similarly, here and there the interpolations "see," "now," "and," "you know," and "you see" have been suppressed, where it is clear they constitute merely articulated pauses or voiced punctuation, rather than in fact being intended substantively as an interjection or a conjunction. Otherwise, all textual deletions have been flagged by the insertion of bracketed ellipses — such deletions generally involving diversions (sometimes brief asides; occasionally extended passages) from the main subject or subjects being treated of in the excerpt or, alternatively, matter duplicative of that present elsewhere within the volume. — E.C.L.

References to the sources of literary quotations not identified within the excerpts themselves

1. from "Magna est Veritas" by Coventry Patmore
2. from "On His Blindness" by John Milton
3. from "An Essay on Man" by Alexander Pope
4. "Man" by Sir John Davies
5. from Sonnet CXVI by William Shakespeare
6. from *As You Like It*, Act II, Scene 7, by William Shakespeare
7. from "To a Mistress Dying" and *The Just Italian*, Act V, Scene 1, by Sir William Davenant
8. from "The Society upon the Stanislaus" by Francis Bret Harte
9. from "Give All to Love" by Ralph Waldo Emerson
10. from "London, 1802," Sonnet XIV of "Poems Dedicated to National Independence and Liberty" by William Wordsworth
11. from the Bible's "Gospel According to St. Mark," 9:24
12. from "Departmental" by Robert Frost
13. from Sonnet XXIX by William Shakespeare
14. from an untitled poem by Walter Savage Landor
15. "The Phoenix" by Arthur Christopher Benson
16. as quoted by Rudyard Kipling from an anonymous song; see his "The Ship That Found Itself," in *The Day's Work*, Part I
17. from the text John Keats specified as an inscription for his tombstone
18. sentiment variously expressed by several writers
19. from "The Song of the Happy Shepherd" by William Butler Yeats
20. from "All Revelation" by Robert Frost
21. from Oenone's song in "The Arrangement of Paris" by George Peele
22. as included in "Mending Wall" by Robert Frost
23. from "Ode" by Arthur William Edgar O'Shaughnessy
24. from "What Fifty Said" by Robert Frost

Index of names, titles, and subjects, as well as of selected key words and phrases, in the main text

189

196

197

The picture featured on the title pages is of Robert Frost speaking at the University of Detroit on November 14, 1962; photograph by Joe Clark, courtesy of the University of Detroit Mercy Library. Those present within the Introduction were taken at Amherst College, October 27, 1955; photographs by D. J. McClune, courtesy of the Amherst College Library.

•

Typesetting by Avanda Peters has been done using Rudoph Ruzicka's Fairfield type. Gill Sans, as used for the titling, was created by Eric Gill. The book has been designed by Roderick D. Stinehour.

The picture featured on the title pages
is of Robert Frost speaking at the University of Detroit on November 14, 1962;
photograph by Joe Clark, courtesy of
the University of Detroit Mercy Library.
Those present within the Introduction
were taken at Amherst College, October
27, 1955; photographs by D. J. McClune,
courtesy of the Amherst
College Library.

•

Typesetting by Avanda Peters has been
done using Rudoph Ruzicka's Fairfield
type. Gill Sans, as used for the titling,
was created by Eric Gill. The book has
been designed by Roderick D. Stinehour.